MA
MAGICK

MAAT MAGICK

A Guide to Self-Initiation

NEMA

Introduction by Kenneth Grant

Foreword by Jan Fries

SAMUEL WEISER, INC.

York Beach, Maine

First published in 1995 by
Samuel Weiser, Inc.
P. O. Box 612
York Beach, ME 03910-0612
www.weiserbooks.com

Library of Congress Cataloging-in-Publication Data

Nema.
    Maat magic : a guide to self-initiation / Nema.
        p.   cm.
    Includes bibliographical references and index.
    1. Magic, Egyptian. 2. Initiation rites. I. Title
BF1591.N46   1995
133.4'3'-032—dc20   95-18084
                                                                CIP
ISBN 0-87728-827-5
BJ

Cover art is a bas-relief of the Goddess Maat, Museo Archeologico,
Florence, Italy. Used by permission of Scala/Art Resource, NY.

Typeset in 11 point Goudy

Printed in the United States of America

09 08 07 06 05 04 03 02 01
10 9 8 7 6 5 4 3 2

CONTENTS

Acknowledgments vii

Introduction by Kenneth Grant ix

Foreword by Jan Fries xiii

Part I: Theory

Maat, the Divine Illusion 3

Level 10 Malkuth/Kingdom 9

Level 9 Yesod/Foundation 17

Level 8 Hod/Splendor 23

Level 7 Netzach/Victory 33

Level 6 Tiphereth/Beauty 43

Level 5 Geburah/Strength 51

Level 4 Chesed/Mercy 59

The Abyss 69

Level 3 Binah/Understanding 75

Level 2 Chokmah/Wisdom 81

Level 1 Kether/Crown 85

Part II: Preshadowing of the Feather

The Coming of a Book 91

Liber Pennae Praenumbra 93

Notes and Comments 101

Part III: Practice

Level 10 Banishments, Feather and Flame
Rite, Consecration 115

Level 9 Mooncup Rite, The Forgotten Ones
Invocation 131

Level 8 Dance of the Mask 145

Level 7 The Mass of Maat 163

Level 6 Invocation of the HGA 169

Level 5 Cosmic Vision, Vortex Ritual 175
Level 4 Pranayama, Adept's Thesis 183
Level 3 Master of the Temple 191
Level 2 The Rite of the Children 197
Level 1 Invocation of the Strange Attractor 207

In Conclusion 217
Glossary 221
Bibliography 229
Index 231
About the Author 238

LIST OF ILLUSTRATIONS

Feather of Maat 4
Altar 10
Astral Temple 20
QBLH–Tree of Maat 26
Invocation 36
Meeting the Angel 46
Camping out 54
N'Aton 64
The Abyss 72
Sixfold Banishment 120
Mooncup 134
The Forgotten Ones 142
Mask Dancer 154
Mass of Maat 166
Being the Angel 172
Vortex 178

ACKNOWLEDGMENTS

Heartfelt thanks and gratitude to

Lyrus Moundbuilder, for musical expertise, suggestions, and support;

Kenneth Grant, for encouragement, editorial help, and Magickal mentoring;

Louis Martinié, for publishing Maat material, editorial help, and longterm friendship;

Donald Michael Kraig, for encouragement and editorial help;

Jan Fries and the European Maat Network, for encouragement and inspiration;

Eric Clarke, Denny Sargent, Rob Carey, Joe Engeleit and Jillian Blum, for *Mandrake*, *Aeon*, and the Horus-Maat Lodge;

Gary Straw, for introducing me to Aleister Crowley;

Lee, Bill, Sue, and Juli, without whom Magick would have been neither possible nor necessary.

To Gwynneth, Jillian, Steven, Andrew, Amanda, and all the children in the world—may they live in it with a wider and deeper consciousness.

INTRODUCTION

Maat was known to the ancient Egyptians as the Goddess of Truth and Justice. The present book concerns a communication from the highest level with special regard to self-initiation into Her Mysteries.

It is difficult to place *Maat Magick* in its true context and perspective without invoking all sorts of seemingly unrelated events which span many decades. It is a very skillfully crafted work, possessing a subtlety and depth not immediately apparent. However, the addition to *Magic* of the letter "*k*" warns us that we are skirting Crowley territory.

Ten years after Crowley's death, in 1947, a batch of letters written by his "magical son," Frater Achad, revealed that the territory was a veritable minefield, and that controversy over the Mysteries of Maat was the fuse which eventually alienated the two men.

Not long before Crowley's death, and totally oblivious to the tension existing between these two great magicians, I asked Crowley when Maat's Aeon would dawn. World War II was grinding to a halt, and contrary to the spirit of general rejoicing, Crowley declared that the war had not yet begun! He was referring, of course, to turbulent years ahead as the Aeon of Horus—inaugurated by his receipt of *The Book of the Law* in 1904—really got underway. A little abashed, I asked again when he thought the Aeon of Maat would appear. He replied, curtly, "Maat can wait." Maat did wait, but not as long, perhaps, as Crowley expected. The year following Crowley's death, that is in 1948, Frater Achad announced the Inauguration of the Aeon of Maat in a series of documents included in the correspondence aforementioned. I studied these documents with some care when, eventually, I came to see them, and Achad's plausible arguments and evidence all but persuaded me that he might be right; but something was lacking. That something was the transmission which Nema, prophetess and the author of this book, received from an extraterrestrial entity named N'Aton, some sixteen years later. It appears in this book as *Liber Pennae Praenumbra*, a simple, straightforward statement possessing none of the torturous complexities inherent in Achad's proclamation; yet it contains profound metaphysical and spiritual implicits. Nema skillfully brings these to the fore, as well as providing a clearcut manual of practical magical working for those with a ceremonial "bent." It is all here; the theory and the practice of a magical culture which, in its fullest development, emerges as a profoundly mystical experience of Truth stripped of every conceivable glamor—of all magick, in fact. None but Nema, writing today, could encompass so vast a range of insights in so forthright a manner.

In a recent letter to me, Nema described her Astral temple: "My Astral Temple (an ankh-shaped sandstone structure) sits on 'the Plain of the Stars'—a desert of sand of pink-lavender (mauve?) color, through which shine a myriad of stars and galaxies. . . . I discovered it in '73."

The description reminded me, inevitably, of an experience shared by members, myself included, of *New Isis Lodge* in 1955, just prior to transmissions from a source we called the Mauve Zone. The experience involved a structure shaped like the astro-glyph of Venus—as near in shape to an ankh sign as made no difference. It was of massive proportions and vertically rooted at a crazy angle in a mauve-hued desert of drifting sand which rippled like water under a steady breeze. Into the top of the sign there flowed three curved streams of light, bluish-white and intensely bright. This sign was eventually modified and adopted by the Lodge as its magical Seal.

It may or may not be significant that we saw in the vast landscape, partially immersed in the sand, what appeared to be several similar structures, their upper parts alone visible. They resembled half-moons with a triple fire-tongue playing on their domes. Nema, who knew nothing about them, was the first person to describe details analogous in respect of the two chief features—the ankh-shaped structure and the color of the desert.

It was owing to the Lodge experience, and the Inner Contacts which it established in its aftermath, that I came to view the structures in the light of receiving-stations or temples of Initiation, although I had not thought of them in connection with Maat. If, indeed, they did have such a connection, then the *New Isis Lodge* stumbled upon a magical zone in which—nearly twenty years later, in 1974—Nema received *Liber Pennae Praenumbra*.

One of the more profound and yet practical lessons to be derived from *Maat Magick* is, surely, that we do not have to "wait" for Maat. For those who live and work NOW in the Light of Maat, Her aeon is already at hand. The concept of successional aeons is shown to be a misconception; we live in the aeon we project all about us, as our "life," as our "world." It follows that as we cease projecting we shall render ourselves available to Maat, Herself. That is our Truth and the Truth of what we ceaselessly project.

Kenneth Grant
London

FOREWORD

In Ancient Egypt, Ma'at was personified as the goddess of truth and justice. Truth! The very idea raises some knotty questions. What is truth? What, more precisely, is your truth? Who are you, and what is your true self? What is your True Will, and how can you do it?

Such questions can accompany people, as their shadows do, through life. Great questions which can upset, confuse, rearrange and enlighten. Questions you can contemplate frequently, and answer occasionally, as suits your mood and work. Though Maat Magick is very concerned with them, it does not pretend to answer them. Truth may seem like a simple idea when observed from a safe distance, but on close quarters it is extremely hard to define.

There are lots of subjective truths in this world, but if there are objective truths, several thousand years of philosophical efforts have failed to reveal them. In my opinion—which is as good as yours and anybody else's—truth depends on the point of view, on the subjective reality of the observer, and on certain conditions, such as time, place, and the will to be done.

If you believe something to be true, this belief is an active force shaping your reality. If you wish to communicate a truth to another, you have to give this truth a form the other can understand. Can you speak truth in the other person's language? If you give shape and form to truth, these are only true for a while. In practice, it can be hard enough to determine just what is true for oneself at a given time, let alone for other people.

This makes Maat Magick a very subtle way of self-discovery. Truth can be a very intimate experience. What was true yesterday need not be true today. Truth changes, just as you do. What will you be like when the Magick of Maat changes you? If you want to find out, here is a book full of inspiration and practice. Nema does not state what Maat is, but offers, as an example, a well-structured series of mind-expanding experiences. Using these rituals and meditations, you can open a gate to the consciousness of Maat, and this is where the fun begins.

Your Self can initiate yourself into Maat.

In recent years, the idea of "self-Initiation" has raised the scorn of many organized cults, orders, and churches, which confer initiations to worthy individuals as a sign of spiritual or financial grace. Have these organizations forgotten that their earliest founders, like the pioneers of many religions and systems of attainment, were largely self-Initiated as well?

Maat Magick, though it emphasizes the idea of being Initiated by one's True Self, should not be classed as a cult or order. If *Maat* means truth, this truth depends on the individual. Who could Initiate another into truth? Who could confer a Grade, a Name, or even a diploma, to testify that someone else is truthful? Who can truly measure the Will and nature of another?

In Maat Magick, you begin on your own and find out about your truth all by yourself. If you want a teacher, ask yourself and listen to the answers. Ask the All-Self, and learn from the world as much as you can.

Nema once wrote that a great way to avoid boredom is to say: "What will the world surprise me with next?" Would you dare to say that? Self goes a long way beyond your personality. You may find the world responding to your call. Not that you stand much of a chance to be bored if you invoke Maat. Access to Maat happens not only in ritual but equally in daily life.

The serious Mages of the last centuries made a distinction between "profane" and "spiritual" activities, and believed in a similar difference between their "Higher Self" and their "ordinary human nature." Many of them divided their daily schedule on this basis, never realizing that their part-time magic only worked during the magical parts of the day.

Nema's work breaks with these traditions of separation. To Maat, and in truth, all aspects of life are equally valid, and each moment is a unique chance to learn, to enjoy, and to work change as you will.

This makes questions of cosmology as important as doing the dishes, and in Nema's Magick, you will find a healthy balance of both.

In one of the first letters I received from her, I was delighted to learn how to change identity using the word "IPSOS," side-by-side with comments on how the peas were growing in the garden. Both ideas are relevant to truth, and join to form a larger vision.

You will notice that Maat Magick uses certain symbols of the Ancient Egyptian religion. This is a matter of convenience. Maat Magick is not necessarily Egyptian magic, unless it is your True Will to practice Egyptian magic.

The True Will is the essential requirement. If your True Will is Wicca, Voodoo, or Tungusian Shamanism, you will find your Maat in that. Quite simply, you can enjoy and practice Maat Magick in any cult or religion, provided you are true to your self.

In this place it may be useful to consider Maat in a historical perspective. Maat was a central concept in the society of Ancient Egypt, and one that endured with few changes as long as Egyptian society did.

Ma'at comes from Mu'at, which derives from the verb M_3 meaning 1) to direct, to steer, to give a direction; 2) to offer, to sacrifice. Maat refers to a mode of organization and a quality of awareness. The word is usually translated as "truth, justice, order, adjustment, honesty." Though the Ancient Egyptians represented Maat as a goddess, there is little "personality cult" to her. Maat was a very abstract concept.

The old idea of Maat described the harmonious relationship among people in society, and with the world around.

From our modern point of view, the society of the Ancient Egyptians was a rigid and conservative theocracy which had little sympathy with innovation and change. To these people, accordance with truth meant practicing the time-honored rituals and "returning to the place of yesterday," to the memory of the origin. In our modern society, which changes faster than anyone can comprehend, Maat requires a very different attitude.

Where the Ancient Egyptian re-lived the rites and regulations of the ancestors, the modern Maat Magician learns from the future as well, and aligns past and future through the word-deeds of the present.

This requires a certain fluid attitude toward identity, and an ability to embrace change that would have seemed unholy to the dwellers of the Nile. In the old times, people believed (or were supposed to) that the well-being of all depended on the principle "acting for others, and others acting for oneself." This phrase is commonly found in Egyptian literature.

One who does well returns to the place of yesterday as it is commanded: do good for him who does good that he may do good. This is to thank him for his doing.

This is to hold back before you shoot.

This is to give tasks to the Lord of Work.[1]

Thus goes the "Peasant's Complaint," a popular poem on the conflict of Maat and corruption, c. 2000 B.C. The essential idea is that as you act for others, others act for you, which makes all activity enlightened self-interest. This Maat regulated not only the relations among people, but also the obligations of humans and gods. "The wage of one who acts is that others act for him. This is the Maat of God."[2]

Here the emphasis lies on activity. It was the doing, the acting in accord with truth and honesty, which was supposed to keep the Egyptian civilization sacred and intact.

By the same mouth it is our doing that shapes the advent of the Aeon of Maat, giving flesh and new meaning to its manifestation.

In old Egypt, people lived in Maat when they ordered their lifestyle in conformity with their caste and its traditions. Modern Magickians have no caste and very few traditions. Instead of regulations, they have a very tricky concept, which postulates that there is such a thing as a self, which is supposed to find and do its True Will. What is the nature of your self? What is the nature of your truth? What is your Maat in relation to the world?

True Will comes to be when self assumes Masks and dances its message.

There is a certain Maat in the way a vulture strengthens its wings, as it rises so easily on a warm air current, spiraling far above the world in steady flight.

---

[1]From the "Peasant's Complaint," a popular poem circa 2000 B.C. Translation by Karlheinz Schüssler, *Märchen und Erzählungen der Alten Ägypter* (Bergisch Gladbach: Gustav Lübbe Verlag GMBH, 1980), p. 30. Another translation is also available by Jan Assmann, *Ma'at, Gerechtigkeit und Unsterblichkeit im Alten Ägypten* (München: Beck Verlag, 1990), Part III, Chapter 1, p. 58; Chapter 2, pp. 60–69.

[2]Inscription in the Osiris Temple, Abydos, circa 1700 B.C.

There is a Maat in the ups and downs in the life of a bat.

There is a Maat in the structure and beauty of a spider's web, as it responds to flies and wind and rain.

There is a Maat in the wisdom of the hive.

There is a Ma'at in the mind that beholds these miracles.

Commonly, the Egyptian culture used two symbols for their Maat idea. One is the well-known feather, bearing a bird (a soul-image) in flight ⨡ .

The feather rides the airways, and air was often associated with Maat. "Maat is breathed," was a common expression, or "Maat gives the air to breathe," while lack of Maat was well known to manifest as "lack of breath," a popular metaphor for oppression, fear, and restriction. Indeed, breath and truth have a lot in common, as you may realize when you do the breathing exercises given in this book. The way you breathe, and truth you believe at the time may influence each other.

The other symbol looks like a flat, horizontal rectangle with a slanted edge to the left ⬜ . It has been interpreted as a ruler, or measuring rod, with the explanation that Maat was the honest measure of the fields.

Now the measuring rods from Egyptian tombs all lack the edge of the symbol. Today, most Egyptologists interpret the symbol as the foundation under the throne, and indeed, such throne foundations occur with some frequency in Egyptian paintings.[3]

In this sense, Maat would be the foundation of the throne, the Earthing that gives validity to the gods. If you like symbolism, please consider that there are two ways up the throne. One way is a step, the other a gradual ascent. As you develop sensitivity for Maat, you may come to recognize that these ways are models of change. We can see evolution as a gradual process, or as a series of distinct steps.

Maat consciousness makes use of both forms of development at once. This book, for instance, offers a way of step-by-step evolution, each stage of development appearing out of the insights and experi-

---

[3]See Wallis E. A. Budge, *The Book of the Dead*. There are various publications of this text available.

ences of the last. This would make Maat Magick a predictable way of attainment. At the same time, it offers access to past and future states of consciousness, which makes the practice unpredictable, indeed. You will soon find that Maat, timeless and ever-present, can connect all times and produce change in more ways than you can imagine.

Whatever you expect, you will be surprised. The foundation below the throne is the Maat of its Earthing. Maat Magick emphasizes Earthing, and reminds us that during our incarnations, our rites begin and end on Earth, with a laugh, a shrug, and a lot to be done.

As the feather lifts awareness to the heights, the Earthing brings the vision into flesh, and forms the world anew. The book you hold in your hands functions equally as feather and foundation.

Maat Magick is the distilled elixir of the hive, a drop of nectar that can change your world. Bees share their nectar, and feed each other, finding communion as they pass the elixir from mouth to mouth. As you partake, pass on what you learn, sharing the secrets of the time-to-be.

By the same mouth,
Jan Fries
Frankfurt/M

PART

I

THEORY

MAAT, THE DIVINE ILLUSION

MAAT IS THE EGYPTIAN *NETER*, GODDESS OF TRUTH, justice, righteousness, measurement and balance. She is depicted as a beautiful young woman wearing a feather, her symbol, in her headband. She is the daughter of Ra, the sun god, and is the wife of Thoth (Tehuti), the ibis-headed scribe of the gods, whom she assisted in the ordering of creation.

In the judgment hall of Osiris, the slain and restored King, the heart of the deceased is placed on one pan of the balance-scale of Anubis, the jackal-headed guide of the dead, and the feather of Maat is in the other. If the heart weighs no more than the feather and is not burdened with sin, the soul goes to Amenta, the Egyptian paradise. If the heart is heavier than the feather, the sinner is devoured by the crocodile god Sebekh, or, in some depictions, by Ammet, a chimera beast.

The term *neter* means "principle," and indicates that the Egyptian Initiates regarded their pantheon, not as gods in the sense of immortal persons to be worshipped, but as ideals and qualities to be honored and practiced.

The Nile's flooding required an annual remeasurement of fields and property lines; truth and justice in measurement were held in high regard as a consequence. This regard for truth extended to ordinary speech and business dealings, as evidenced in the Negative Confession of the Papyrus of Nu:

> . . . I have not done iniquity.
> . . . I have not made light the bushel.

FEATHER OF MAAT

... I have not acted deceitfully.

... I have not uttered falsehood.

... I have not set my mouth in motion against any man.

... I have not made myself deaf unto the words of right and truth.

... I have not multiplied my speech beyond what should be said."[1]

There are a total of 42 sins listed in the Negative Confession, many of which are related to truth. Maat is the most abstract of the *neter*, a perfect patron for the true goal of Magick.

Aleister Crowley defines Magick as "the Science and Art of causing Change to occur in conformity with Will."[2] This is a wide definition that encompasses all purposeful actions. In practice, Magick is a way of life that includes ethics, philosophy, scholarship in various fields, ritual meditation, devotion, divination, and discipline.

Contrary to the popular concept, Magick's aim is not to violate or suspend the laws of Nature in order to produce miracles on the physical plane, but to transform the Magickian through the process of initiation. Initiation is a series of stages of realization that expand your vision of reality beyond the physical, mental, and emotional planes, and include the spiritual, the divine and their transcendence.

The physical manifestations that often occur during this expansion are unimportant side effects and shouldn't be allowed to distract you from the course of initiation. These include various PSI phenomena, synchronicities, serendipities, apparitions, and hunches.

Magick transcends the ability of organized religions to unite the soul with God, inasmuch as it is an individual endeavor of direct experience, unmediated by an official priesthood, and independent of dogma, doctrine, and dependency on faith. Magick's initiations provide you with experience, not hearsay, with knowledge instead of faith.

The Magickian has a treasure in the writings and traditions of past seekers of truth; the ethics of the High Art require that each ini-

---

[1] Sir E. A. Wallis Budge, *Egyptian Religion* (New York: Bell Publishing Co., 1959), pp. 156–160.

[2] Aleister Crowley, *Magick in Theory and Practice* (New York: Castle Books, ND), p. xii.

tiate share the findings, experiences, and conclusions with the initiated community through time and space. The body of initiated tradition is a tool and not a restriction; knowledge of a wide range of experiences and methodologies provides a solid base for one's own adventures and means for comparing new encounters with those of other practitioners. Magick includes all of its history in itself, from the spirit-journeys of the shaman and the animism of pre-civilized peoples, through the patient observations of astrologers and alchemists, the elaborate medieval rituals of Ceremonial Magick to contemporary experimental practices.

The Magickian studies and learns from science, religion, and art, all of which were part of the High Art in the past. Contemporary science restricts itself to the physically measurable and mathematically predictable; contemporary religion restricts itself to matters of faith and morals, for the most part, save for fundamentalist literalists. Art, in its many forms, approaches Magick in its individuality and its expression of wordless realizations; art seeks to abolish restriction of vision and method.

Although anyone of sufficient intelligence can practice Magick, few people do. Magick remains occult (hidden) from the satisfied, the complacent, the content. The rigors of the High Art are so demanding and dangerous that only the most determined seeker will choose its pursuit. When the views of life we are taught by family, church, school, and society fail to convince or satisfy us, we have no choice but to explore life on our own, passing beyond the ordinary and the obvious.

Maat Magick has more than one aim in its intent. First is the transformation of the Magickian into the realized Self; second is the transformation of the human race into its next evolutionary stage; third is the preparation of our species to meet and understand nonhuman intelligence and events beyond our present accumulated experience.

How does Maat, an ancient Egyptian *neter*, fit in a future-oriented Magickal system? My introduction to Magick was through the writings of Aleister Crowley, who divided human time into Aeons characterized by particular Egyptian *neter*.

The Aeon of Isis was the time of the mother-goddess, of integration with Nature in hunter-gatherer societies, of a reverence for fertility and clan. The Aeon of Osiris was the time of the father-god, of the conquest of Nature in city-building and migrating societies, of a reverence for wealth and power. The Aeon of Osiris brought the phenomena of government, organized religion, slavery, war, and money.

In 1904, Aleister Crowley proclaimed the advent of the Aeon of Horus, the Crowned and Conquering Child, come to destroy the wrongs and excesses of the Osirian Aeon. The major Western manifestation of Osiris as the slain and risen god is Christianity, a religion of submission and dependency on a divine incarnation. The submission and dependency were transferred to Church, State, and class system. By Crowley's time, repression and hypocrisy were the norm for social and personal behavior.

The Aeon of Horus, the hawk-headed Lord of Force and Fire, manifested the first stage of change in the Western *zeitgeist* with the first of the World Wars, and continues today.

Although the Child is the synthesis of the Mother and Father dialectic, there was a fourth factor needed to complete the family of Aeons, to complete the Magickal formula* of IHVH*[3] where I (Yod) is the father, H (Hé) is the mother, V (Vau) is the son, and the final H (Hé) is the daughter.

This fourth factor is Maat, and her Aeon is in effect in tandem with the Aeon of Horus. The female form of Maat links with the infant male form of Heru-Pa-Kraat (Harpocrates), god of silence. HPK is the child Horus and is seen by some as the patron and namesake of the Aeon following that of Ra-Hoor-Khut, the martial form of Horus. It's profitable to meditate on the relationship between silence and truth.

The martial Horus destroys the crippling remnants of past institutions and philosophies; Maat builds and delineates the shape of our social and individual world-in-formation. *Maat Magick* invokes the principle of truth in this formation of the future and our descendants. All six aspects of the Magickal current are available for present workings.

Under the Biblical idea of "dominion" over Nature, Western society has abused the planet we live on in countless ways. Part of

---

[3]Asterisks indicate words found in glossary.

Maat Magick, part of becoming our next stage as a species, lies in the healing of our planetary ecology through integrating ourselves as the Earth's neurosystem, and changing our physical behavior in our relationship with the mineral, vegetable, and animal kingdoms.

Many Neopagans and Wiccans are ecological activists, as are those without labels who have seen the toxic condition of our environment. Magickians, on the other hand, have focused, traditionally, on the transphysical realms of the astral planes and the realm of Jungian archetypes. Maat Magick concerns the entire realm of existence, Outer and Inner; knowledge and power demand responsibility. Magick is not an escape from any part of life, but a synthesis of the whole.

Maat Magick arises from and is a form of Thelemic Magick, the system of initiation formulated by Crowley. Although it's useful to be familiar with Thelema, you can practice Maat Magick with no experience in other systems except your own. The only requirement for success in Maat Magick is that you be in the process of discovering your True Will. I do suggest extensive reading of Crowley's writings, however.

Maat Magick draws on Western and Eastern traditions and methods. Anything useful is fair game—Qaballah, mantra meditation, tarot, yoga, astrology, tantra, Voodoo, shamanic journeys, quantum physics, astral travel, genetics, cosmology, trance work, chaos theory, etc. Maat/truth is eternal and flexible, assuming contradictory guises according to the capacity of the beholder.

Maat touches all concerns in life: survival, independence, family situations, love, hate, jealousy, fear, illness, death, eternity, loneliness, purpose, and choices. There is no situation that cannot be improved by an infusion of truth, even though the process is often painful.

No one comes to Magick without a profound dissatisfaction with ordinary answers, conventional wisdom, the traditional institutions of society and one's own thoughts. The essence of initiation lies beyond all naturally-occurring means of realization, and yet, once attained, seems plainly obvious.

I have presented Theory and Practice in separate sections of this book so the reader encounters all of the former before doing any of the latter.

LEVEL 10

MALKUTH / KINGDOM

THOSE FAMILIAR WITH THE TREE OF LIFE WILL RECOG-
nize the structure of the levels of density I use here. I thank my colleague, Frater Priba, for the concept and his permission to use it.

There are ten Levels of existence in Western tradition, ranging
from the familiar physical world our bodies inhabit to the edges of
Nothing. Physical existence is the tenth and densest Level.

Even at its densest, the physical world is built from the most
tenuous of subatomic particles that are interacting wave-packets of
energy. For practical purposes, we'll consider ourselves and our environment as solid and tangible.

In the history of spiritual seeking, there have been those who
hold matter to be intrinsically evil, or to be a snare and temptation
to be renounced for the sake of spirit. This view of matter in general
as evil arose from the distractions from spirituality provided by sex,
greed, and violent emotions. Sex is the leading distraction, since it's
the strongest and most intimate of the survival urges after hunger
(which includes thirst).

Maat regards the material world as holy, worthy of respect and
love, and the realm in which all Magick must manifest to be complete. Magick is doing, not talking about or thinking about the
changes we Will to occur. Magickal practice begins and ends in the
tenth level of density.

In practice, you establish a temple space and an altar, acquire
your Magickal tools (wand, sword, cup, and pantacle), obtain your ritual robe and various other objects (such as candles, incense, essential

ALTAR

oils, drums, bells, and appropriate pictures and statues). The more of these things you can make yourself, the better. All are consecrated and dedicated to the High Art of Magick, though the temple space can be a corner of a bedroom, attic, or basement, or a secluded spot in the woods.

The establishment of a physical work room (temple) and work bench (altar) is a common feature of all ritualists, be they Magickians, Witches, general Neopagans or members of variations of established religions worldwide. Any and all of the traditional objects and spaces can be reinterpreted and updated with appropriate technology, as long as correspondences are clear. There is a consecration/dedication ritual in the Practice Section of this book.

If you are just beginning your Magickal practice, I strongly suggest that you perform a banishing ritual at the beginning of any ritual, or meditation, before you go to sleep each night, and upon awakening each day. Since Magick is a way of life, you can speed its establishment as such by making each act you do a willed, consecrated act. There are a number of banishing rituals in initiated tradition, which it would benefit you to research. I've included two Maat Magick banishments in the Practice Section.

There are several reasons for doing banishments, each reason based in a density Level from 10 through 6. It's well to remember that the ten-level divisions of existence are an arbitrary, but convenient means of mapping a seamless continuum. Conditions, entities, and characteristics of one level can act and appear in neighboring levels in many ways.

In Level 10, a banishment dedicates a specific space and time to Magickal work, clears away interference and concentrates the Magickian's attention on the work at hand. I suggest the complete banishment for beginners, since they shine like beacons on the astral planes (Level 9) and draw all sorts of lower-astral beings looking for life-force.

Every healthy human being lives on all ten levels of the continuum of existence, even though most of us are unaware, in waking consciousness, of levels more rarefied than Levels 9 or 8. When you take the first actions to begin your Magickal practice, you activate your conscious participation in Level 9. The presence of your conscious attention there attracts the notice of the "natives": ghosts, dreams, nightmares, unresolved negative emotions, psychic vampires (who often have physical bodies—you know them by how they drain you), interdimensional alien monsters, primitive survival urges, Black Lodges, etc.

When you do a thorough banishment, you ward out all such entities from your dedicated spacetime, while simultaneously shielding your neighbors from the energies you raise in your work and the effects such energies have on people and events. Banishments can be done to clean out and dedicate a house, apartment, office, automobile—any structure or place that needs it.

You can carry a protective field about you as you move through your daily life. After you've banished a spacetime for ritual, meditation, or any other purpose, and when the working is completed, imagine the boundaries of the space shrinking around you until it fits your form. This practice is useful in temporarily insulating your developing "extra-senses" from information overload, and in insulating your increasing energy from detection by undesirables.

Banishing on Level 10 has another good aspect, which is being a minor First Initiation Ordeal. Most initiations in the denser levels are preceded or accompanied by ordeals.

There once was a farmer who owned a mule that resisted being trained to harness or plow. The farmer went to town and hired a muleskinner to train the mule: the muleskinner agreed to come to his farm the following day. As the farmer approached the corral the next morning, he saw the muleskinner swing a length of two-by-four and bash the mule between the ears.

"What do ya think you're doing?" yelled the farmer. "I hired you to train that mule, not kill 'im!"

"I *am* trainin' him, Mister," said the muleskinner. "I just have to get his attention first."

Ordeals are designed to get your attention, to give you an often intense motive, to provide a koan-in-action so you open to a changed point of view. The changed view, the new realization, constitutes the initiation.

For the beginner, the ordeal of doing a banishment consists of embarrassment about speaking aloud, moving about in a strangely decorated place, wearing a robe or going nude, and making odd gestures, even in solitude. Not only is it necessary to engage in foolish actions, it's necessary to be sincere and totally involved in the process. If any Magickal working is done superficially, tentatively, or as camp, it will fail and possibly backfire on the Magickian.

On Level 9, a banished spacetime functions as a stable home base amid a flowing and fluctuating landscape; it keeps your attention free from the distractions of the astral planes.

On Level 8, banishment helps quiet the ongoing chattering of the mind. We rarely notice the continuous monologue of rationalization our mind delivers to us, but it goes on until we learn the art of silence. Silence grows from the regular practice of mantra meditation and pranayama (breathing discipline), but the beginnings of silence can be aided by banishment.

On Level 7, banishment dissolves habit, prejudice and comfortable associations of symbols and metaphors. It creates space for a new appreciation of nature and human nature, and frees the imagination to translate and transmit new experience in various forms of art.

Banishment on Level 6 centers you in the sacred spacetime, centers the sacred spacetime in the universe at large, and gives you a place to stand from which to move the world. In performing the banishment ritual, you gather the reins and responsibility of Magickal power into your hands. You alone have the authority to act in the area you've banished (an authority you can share with colleagues in group workings), and you alone must answer for the results of your actions.

With growing experience, you'll find that the abridged form of banishments work to trigger the necessary ritual conditions and centering. The universe provides immediate feedback when a Magickian acts prematurely; you'll know when it's appropriate to forego the longer forms.

In addition to the daily practice of banishing, it's important to meditate regularly; ideally, twice a day in twenty to thirty minute sessions. I've found that mantra meditation works well for the practice of silence and no-mind.

Mantra meditation is the form of the Feather and Flame Ritual, which is the main means of establishing your link with the Maat current. There is a general Magickal Current flowing through the universe, from the Big Bang to the Big Crunch. Each Aeon and its Word imprints its characteristic frequency/signal on the general Current, tuning it to the level of the complexity of consciousness available among humanity at the time. The Feather and Flame ritual is in the Practice Section.

Magick is a circuit. You explore each level of decreasing density until you learn enough about and through a given level to bring your new realizations back to Level 10 in use and practice. The return to Level 10 is called "Earthing your Magick"; without it, your circuit remains open and no power flows through to do the work.

Both banishing and meditating are Earthing activities, inasmuch as your body gestures and your mouth speaks words, or your body sits still for a period of time and slows its breathing in sympathy with the depths of consciousness you reach with your mantra. All physical ritual is a form of Earthing, in that your physical body moves about and your mouth speaks audible words.

Another, and perhaps more important sense of Earthing, lies in applying your new way of looking at life in your daily actions. This anchors your attainments and establishes them as a permanent part of yourself. It also begins the process of changing the world around you in conformity with Will.

The Magickomystical process, then, is: your awareness ascends the levels of density to a level of greater rarity than Level 10; you acquire new information on that rarer level; the information provides, or you create, a ritual that will express the information on Level 10. You perform the ritual; you record the details; you apply the principles of the new information in your daily life; record results or lack of same; share your findings with your colleagues, in person, on screen, or in print. Repeat the process—and try out the rituals of your colleagues. Share your findings with the creative ritualist(s).

Magick can and does work at a distance through space and time via the quantum connection* of all existence. Magick can influence other people and events through talismans and Magickal Links. The primary means of manifesting Magick in the world of Level 10, however, remains the Magickian's. You are the strongest and most authorative translator of your own visions; as you express them in art or in ordinary living, you launch ripples of change in your environment. A single act or encounter in Level 10, if done precisely in terms of aim, power, and aptness, can trigger a cascade of events that have far-ranging effects, sometimes of global magnitude. There are four basic kinds of rituals:

—Daily practice and discipline rites for the development of the Magickian's strength, sensitivity, centering and openmindedness.

—Seasonal celebration rituals to mark the stations on the Wheel of the Year at the Solstices and Equinoxes, the cross-quarters (October 31, February 2, April 30, and August 1) and significant anniversaries. These serve to orient you to the spacetime conditions of Level 10, and permit you to utilize the energies and forms most harmonious with the time.

—Initiatory or information-seeking rituals. These include ritual elements of reception, like trances, divination, meditational no-mind, and invocations of godforms and forces. This type of ceremony confirms the preparation of the Magickian to receive new information and issues a formal invitation to the information desired.

—Priestly or community rituals. In these rites, you act as an assistant or facilitator for those who want to mark a life-passage or a major decision with a ceremony of some formality. This type of rite includes handfastings, healings, "paganing," or dedicating a newborn to spirituality, wakes and funerals, puberty celebrations, house banishings and blessings, etc.

Magickians are often seen to be lone wolves or members of Magickal orders that are traditionally ranked into grades or degrees. The Magickian has a reputation of being aloof and remote, a figure of mystery rather than a figure of warmth—like a Wiccan High Priestess or High Priest. This image is a false one; Magickians are as integrated with society as anyone else.

Maat sees three levels of Magickal competence: Initiate, Adept, and Priest. The Initiate is busy learning the realities behind appearances; the Adept is busy assisting these realities to appear; the Priest assists others to comprehend reality through direct experience.

As you ascend the levels of diminishing density/increasing rarity, you become familiar with them, learning their truths and rules of operation. Your initiatory competence advances accordingly, as do your concerns and interests. There are several daily practices beyond meditation and banishment that I've found helpful in establishing a good grounding in Level 10.

—*Liber Resh vel Helios* by Aleister Crowley. Performed four times a day at sunrise, noon, sunset, and midnight, this oration to the Sun reminds you of your base in space and time while directing your attention to the Solar energies of Level 6.

—Food Magick. This consists of selecting, preparing, and eating food with awareness of its origins and virtues and of charging it with Magickal energy to vitalize yourself and your fellow diners. It also keeps you mindful of your place on the food chain.[*1]

—The Ganges Oration. I use this in all watery circumstances: taking a drink, washing hands, dishes, clothes, floors, etc., walking or driving over a bridge that crosses a river or stream, taking a bath or a shower, swimming, etc.

"Hail to thee, O Mother Ganges, who flows ever around the world and returns ever to thy source. Purify us now I pray thee, for the ongoing ritual of life. *Hare hare* Ganga.

—The keeping of a Magickal Record. Don't even *think* about relying on your memory alone to record the information and events that initiation brings. A standard spiral notebook and a ballpoint pen or a pencil are all you need. Write in it every day, as a matter of discipline. Record anything you judge pertinent to your Magick—new concepts learned, rituals performed, results observed, inspirations, visions, etc. Your Magickal record is your best friend.

With comprehension of the principles of Level 10, you should be able to set yourself a regimen of practices to help your own initiatory progress.

---

[1]Thanks, compadre Louis Martinié.

YESOD / FOUNDATION

EXISTENCE ON LEVEL 9 IS MORE FLUID THAN ON LEVEL 10, though there are many correspondences among forms native to both levels. Space, time, and the objects within them behave differently, are more elastic and subject to quicker changes than on the material level of density.

Part of Level 9 has been called the Astral Planes. Sleeping dreams occur here, as do daydreams and directed (lucid) dreaming. The latter practice is also called envisoning, imagining, or imaging, and constitutes an important part of Magick. To make Magick, the Mage must imagine the image of desire; the linguistic connections bespeak a reality.

Change occurs constantly in the universe, with or without human knowledge or approval. In order to *cause* "change to occur in conformity with Will," you need a conscious awareness of your desired change, in as much detail, depth, and texture as possible. Vague wishes and vaporous generalities carry no power and don't know how to manifest.

I recommend the building of your Astral Temple as a good training project. In its course, you'll acquire a working space on Level 9, you'll strengthen your powers of visualization and perception, and you'll come to recognize your own style of imaging. It's important that you can recognize your own products and projections, that you're utterly familiar with the characteristics of the images you create, so you can recognize strange astral forms when you encounter them. It could be argued that you create all astral imagery you perceive, but this isn't true on Level 9. Besides the Jungian Racial Unconscious, there are individual and group entities that are definitely not yourself in this sphere.

Although each individual has a small personal vestibule on Level 9, your personal astral space opens on a vast common area, akin to fictional cyberspace that is shared by all, human and otherwise.

Before you seek contact with astral beings, or do any traveling in the common space, it's well to construct your temple in your personal vestibule.

Begin by conducting a banishment in your temple on Level 10, while envisioning yourself saying the same words and doing the same actions in a blank gray fog. After the banishment, seat your physical body comfortably but remain standing in Level 9.

Notice the pressure growing against the soles of your feet as the fog solidifies beneath them. It rises in little wisps and curls about your ankles until you determine the landscape in which your temple is to be erected. Once you've picked a setting, look down and notice that the fog is gaining color, texture, and solidity in a wave radiating from beneath your feet. Sand grains shift and slide, grasses flutter in a breeze, rocks rise and tumble toward a mountain slope, roots twist from forest giants, or wind-blown waves foam up a silty beach. On the astral planes, you can shape your environment in any way you choose. You can site your temple anywhere you can imagine, from familiar places on this planet, on the moon or another planet, or in places impossible on Level 10.

For instance, my own Astral Temple is located on the Plain of Stars, where the lavender sands are shining in their depths with far stars and galaxies, and where it's always sunrise.

Your Astral Temple can be a castle or a cave, a hut, or a fortress; the only limit is your own taste and ability. Establish the details of your environment in as many sessions as it takes to be clear. Lay in your foreground, midground, and background features in a sphere around you, a sphere that has no boundaries when you're inside it. Set your atmosphere, sky, and lighting, if any. Let distant features fade into a horizon or haze, give midground features the same degree of clarity you have in your Level 10 sight, and make foreground features detailed and textured. Every time you enter this astral space, take the time to see that everything is as you've made it. This reinforces the strength of the image; if you notice changes in your environment that you didn't consciously make, you can check for intruders or messages. It's a good idea to write a detailed description of your Astral Temple in your Magickal Record.

Once you've established your surroundings, it's time to begin building the temple, itself. One approach is to imagine a mass that's shaped roughly in the form of your structure, then add details by thinking them into existence. You can sculpt the mass with the ease of thought. It's a good idea to complete the exterior of the temple before shaping its interior.

Another method is to envision the building materials, then levitate the stones, mortar, tiles, etc., into place. For a truly rococo approach, you can envision into being a whole crew of workers with tools, and create a set of blueprints for your imaged construction boss. The major problem with this idea is that astral constructs take on a life of their own and gain independence from their creator. It's better to do the work yourself and have your temple the way you want it.

It's also possible to visualize your temple as completely formed. Move yourself around it to establish it in detail on all sides, top and bottom. On Level 9, you can interpenetrate objects and entities with your astral body, fly, hover, dive underground without tunneling, and change locale with the speed of thought. Take time to become familiar with every external feature of your temple and fix it in your memory.

Once the exterior of your temple is firmly established, open its doorway and walk inside. Form the floor, walls, ceiling, and furnishings according to your taste. Since the astral planes are flexible, you can have the inside of the temple larger than the outside, if you so prefer. Again take your time to do a thorough job on the interior. In Maat Magick, it's helpful to include a feather somewhere in the furnishings.

In the course of constructing your temple, include an interface with the common astral region. This could be a doorway, a large Magick Mirror, a transporter deck—some kind of opening according

ASTRAL TEMPLE

to your taste, large enough for you to pass through, and able to be secured against unauthorized entry.

When you've completed the interior of your Astral Temple, perform a rite to link your astral tools and altar with your physical tools and altar. You could repeat the rituals in your physical temple, or do them in your Astral Temple and in your physical temple simultaneously.

Once you have your Astral Temple, use it regularly. Although it's good to do your rituals on Levels 10 and 9 simultaneously, you can use your Astral Temple when you're away from your physical one. Your physical body can be sitting quietly with its eyes closed while your astral body is dancing and chanting in ritual on Level 9 in its temple.

A word of warning: don't let this Level 9 capacity make you lazy on Level 10. Magick has to be earthed to be complete, and "emergency" astral work needs a physical token sooner or later. There are some students of the High Art who "only work on the astral," as they put it. This is a contradiction in terms, and a thinly-disguised excuse armchair Magickians use to rationalize their lack of real work.

Now that you have your temple established on Level 9, and have it attuned to your physical temple, there is a logical sequence in its use. For those who are exploring Level 9 for the first time, it's wise to use a Magick Mirror, crystal ball, or other scrying means on Level 9. It could be a reflecting pool in your temple courtyard, a great window facing the astral common space, a wall-sized thin-screen TV, a classic bronze mirror, or any image that meets your needs. On Level 10, always keep your Magickal Record at hand when you work on Level 9.

Devise your own method for activating your scrying device and remain in no-mind while watching it. You can simply activate it, then wait to see what appears, or you can call specific images appropriate to a given concept, such as an astrological sign, or a godform, or a principle, etc. Create a symbol, or use one from tradition and send it through your scrying device into the common space.

When the images give you information, write it down in your Magickal Record, along with a thorough description of the image: nature, color, background, your internal impressions and responses.

Ask for a name or a number as identification from the communicating entity and record it for later analysis.

In your first explorations of Level 9, work within your temple, scrying through your instruments and coordinating with your Level 10 rituals by performing them simultaneously on Level 9. When you meditate on Level 10, do so on Level 9 also. At bedtime, enter your Astral Temple as you fall asleep, and record your dreams in your Magickal Record immediately upon awakening.

Initiation is not a guarantee of sainthood, nor is it hazard-free. There may be occasions when you feel that you're under astral attack, either from natives of Level 9, or from someone trying to reach you through the astral commons.

For anonymous sources, envision yourself surrounded by a diamond-hard aura, a hard egg-shape impenetrable by anything outside of yourself, but open to your own purposes. Seal it with the symbols of the Eye of Horus and the Feather of Maat by imagining them glowing in your heart chakra.

When you know the source, write the name on a piece of paper, place it between two small mirrors facing each other and wrap them in aluminum foil, shiny side in. At the same time, envision the person (or thing) encased in a mirrored egg, also sealed with the Eye of Horus and the Feather of Maat. As a final touch, follow the advice of Aleister Crowley and go to a comedy movie and dissolve the situation in laughter.

As you gain experience on Level 9, you can expand your range of activites by venturing into the astral commons in your own form, or in that of an animal or bird, visit far places on Level 10 through the commons, or speak with the dead. We die a second time when we leave our astral bodies in the same way as we've left our physical bodies at physical death. Some people linger in Level 9, for one reason or another, past the usual forty days; there are times when we can help the fearful in their release.

There are further operations on Level 9 that are appropriate after attaining initiation on rarer levels. Level 9 is the staging area for shaping the manifestations determined by work on the higher levels. It deserves enough of your time and effort to gain familiarity with it.

HOD / SPLENDOR

AS THE NINTH LEVEL OF DENSITY DEALS WITH DREAMS, images, and instincts, Level 8 is home to concepts, reasoning, logic, and clarification. Numbers and their relationships are native to Level 8, as are the scientific method and the study of Qabalah, the relationship of the meaning of words to numbers.

Study and experiment are vital to the practice of Magick. Making allowances for the vocabularies of times past, and the worldviews that shaped them, you can discern eternal truths that appear in all the writings of Initiated Tradition. The most important thing to guard against in your reading of the Initiated Tradition is literalism. Biblical fundamentalists are literalists. They "confuse the planes" by treating metaphors and symbols as straight description.

It's easy for the Magickal neophyte to fall into the same trap. The miracles of legendary Mages, such as Merlin, suspend or break physical law; Simon Magus attempts to fly; the Sorcerer's Apprentice can't stop his animated brooms, and Aleister Crowley turns Victor Neuburg into a camel.

Right.

These things are true on Levels 9, 8, or 7, but not on Level 10. As I've mentioned, the levels of density we're discussing are classifications imposed on a continuum, and the aspects of one level can act on other levels. Such is the case with PSI talent, which works on the interzone between Levels 9 and 10. Magick uses, rather than breaks or suspends, the laws of nature, but we don't know all the laws yet. It's only relatively recently that secular science has admitted the observer's role in the experiment.

All of which means that the information available in the Initiated Tradition needs to be read with an eye to the meanings behind the words, and with the assurance that your accumulated experience in the practice of Magick will increase your interpretative abilities and the scope of your understanding. Be as broad and deep in your studies as you can be; keep abreast of the latest findings and theories of secular science, stay in tune with world and local news and music, become aware of contemporary artists of all fields, and their concerns and their statements.

Introspection under invocation of Maat, or honest self-study, is an important part of initiatory work on Level 8. Your mind needs to observe, not only the rest of your aspects, but also its own workings. Set your mind tasks that test its limits: follow chains of cause and effect backward to find the ultimate cause of any event; seek out the connection among phenomena, ask the big philosophical questions.

You'll notice in this level that your mantra meditation serves to quiet the mind's incessant chatter and leaves it open. The mind's silence is necessary for it to receive new information without prejudice. Mental prejudice consists of trying to make new data conform to accepted concepts and rejecting anything that doesn't fit.

When you begin investigating the various branches of Initiated Tradition, you'll notice how Qabalah ties in with the tarot, how both tie in with astrology, alchemy, Voodoo and runes, and how all of them tie in with your own observations.

One aspect of Qabalah is Gematria, the art of determining the number of a word, and its relationship with other words of the same number. The Hebrew letters have numerical values, and the sum of the letter-values in a word is the number-value of a word. Words which share the same, or related numbers share spiritual or Magickal qualities.

There are several versions of an English Qabalah, where numbers are assigned to the letters of the alphabet, and some initiates find them useful. I prefer transliterating words by sound into the

Hebrew, since there is an existing reference table of correspondences in *Sepher Sephiroth*[1]* with which to make immediate comparisons, and the letters have traditional number values. Working the English Qabalah requires you to compile your own table of words with matching number values. The same holds true for any language. Such a pursuit has attracted many initiates, even to the point of obsession.

For my own purposes, Gematria serves to verify, to a certain extent, names and Words of Power received in vision or trance. This is one of the reasons to keep thorough notes in your Magickal Record on information you find on Level 9. It's always a good idea to seek a name or word from the source of a vision or from any entity that appears in a vision.

If the given word works out to have a number listed in *Sepher Sephiroth* with other words that relate to the nature of the information contained in the vision, you can accept the information as probably true.

Qabalah has a schematic chart of existence called the Tree of Life, consisting of ten spheres and 22 paths. The spheres are congruent with the levels of density we're discussing here; the paths relate to the trump cards, or Atus, of the tarot deck, and each relates to a Hebrew letter. There are a plethora of versions of the tarot available today, many of them with a particular spiritual slant, or point of view. I recommend the Thoth Deck, and *The Book of Thoth*,*[2] by Aleister Crowley, and *The New Orleans Voodoo Tarot*,*[3] for the serious seeker.

Each tarot card has an elemental or astrological correlation, as well as an alchemical significance. In the small cards, each elemental suit has three cards for each sign of the element, except the Aces. The court cards have double elemental references, and the trumps represent the Zodiacal signs, the elements, and the planets.

---

[1]Aleister Crowley, *777 and Other Qabalistic Writings*, Israel Regardie, editor (York Beach, ME: Samuel Weiser, 1970).
[2]Aleister Crowley, *The Book of Thoth* (York Beach, ME: Samuel Weiser, 1969).
[3]Louis Martinié and Sallie Ann Glassman, *The New Orleans Voodoo Tarot* (Rochester, VT: Destiny Books, 1992).

QBLH—TREE OF MAAT

Tarot cards are popularly used for divination or fortune-telling, but their value to the initiate lies far beyond this. The seventy-eight cards of the tarot are a book, or rather, the chapter headings of a book. The cards are also an alphabet, and a language of communication among the levels of density of yourself and the universe. The Tree of Life is also a language.

In Maat Magick, the Dance of the Mask is the crafting of artificial personalities, or masks, based on the tarot trumps/paths of the tree/planets and signs of the Zodiac. The masks are danced, or worn, by the Magickian in private conversations, at parties, on the job, giving speeches and doing ritual. For the most part, the trumps describe positions of initiatory responsibility, appropriate actions and/or diagnoses of situations.

In any relationship of teaching, sharing information, or counseling, the person with the information to convey has the responsibility of speaking the psychological language of the recipient. The Dance of the Mask gives you a complete wardrobe of personalities. After you are sure of the other person's nature and disposition, select the mask that the person is most likely to trust, and put it on. Give yourself enough time to immerse yourself in the mask, then dance it. His/her censors won't be able to block the reception of the information you give, if you're nimble and artful enough to dance around them.

Your Daily Mask, or natural personality, grows in texture and depth in your experiences with the masks of the dance. After a sufficient period of dancing the mask as a formal working, you'll find yourself automatically speaking the other person's psychological language without having to think about it.

You'll notice that each level of density has its own vocabulary and that you generally function, in mask, as a translator of a truth from a rarer level to a denser level. This can begin from Level 8, relatively dense as it is, because you have a responsibility to our species as an initiate. This does not mean badgering family and friends with self-defined superiority, nor being darkly mysterious and sinister, nor being any kind of missionary. Subtlety and delicacy is the order of the day. The only way to Dance the Mask successfully is to remember that behind the mask there is no dancer, only dance.

Commentary on the 22 masks is in the Practice Section of this book.

Level 8 concerns itself with science. The present body of information available to the human race is so vast and voluminous that we rely on each other as specialists. There are generalists who translate the work of the specialists into language understood by the general public—Stephen Hawking, Carl Sagan, and Isaac Asimov (R.I.P) come to mind.

Magickians need grounding in a lay understanding of contemporary science. The more we know about the physical universe and the way events happen, the better we can use that way in causing our changes to happen. "That which is above is like that which is below; that which is below is like that which is above," says the Emerald Tablet of Hermes Trismegistus.

The Magickian uses symbols, metaphors, and a certain amount of PSI talent in making Magick work; so does the scientist in making science work. Scientists aim to confine their interest and attention to Level 10, for the most part; the Magickian does not.

The new entities discovered by science, such as black holes, quarks, and fractals, and manifested through technology, such as genetic engineering, global communication and virtual reality, can be used as symbols, metaphors and Magickal Links for PSI force. It's legitimate use for scientific discoveries to be applied in Magick on various levels without earning the label pseudoscience. There are congruous patterns of consciousness for each level, resonant octaves and harmonics, for every fact or idea expressed in Level 10.

Traditional Magick uses terms and forms derived from oral history and myth, anthropomorphic or zoomorphic pantheons, and Holy Books such as the Bible, Koran, Vedas, Sutras, etc.

Maat Magick uses these assets, but also seeks out scientific concepts based on new, better, and more numerous data. The old myths drew their power from the number of people who were familiar with them and admired them. The new scientific concepts draw their power from the number of people who are familiar with them and admire them. The rapidity of modern electronic communications enables discoveries and new ideas to be known around the world within minutes of their announcement.

It's logical to use those symbols which best reflect Level 10 reality in working Magick to be manifested in Level 10. This calls into action the traditional laws of similarity and contagion of Sympathetic Magick. For example: if you decide to take a bio-PSI approach to assisting the Maat mutation from *Homo sapiens* to *Homo veritas*, you might consider using nanotechnology as your working metaphor or viewpoint. It'd be useful to have a picture of the DNA double helix, or gene map, and a simple machine-form drawing. Its form must be able to hold an electric charge capable of molecular adjustment; it should include electrodes for precision application of the charge.

Construct a sigil from the letters N, A, T, O, and N, then copy the sigil on the drawing of the machine. Envision the machine, with its sigil and in three solid dimensions, sitting on your astral altar. Look at the picture of the DNA molecule, and adjust the size of the machine so that it's 1/20th the size of the DNA, at which point we can call the machine a nanon. Hold the image of the nanon and its sigil firmly in mind while you charge it by whatever method you choose. Command the nanon to replicate and watch it grow into a sparkling horde of purposeful billions. Call the horde to the doorway of your Astral Temple and send them flying into the commons, with a command to seek those who are willing to change.

The astral nanons will circle the globe with the speed of thought; when welcomed, they enter the individual and home in on certain neurons in the brain. Sliding through membranes and cytoplasm, the nanon enters the nucleus, locates the appropriate segment of genes, and awakens certain among them with a gentle electric buzz—all on Level 9. The activation of a dormant gene on Level 9 activates its counterpart on Level 10. On Level 10, the awakened gene creates RNA keys to a cascade of chemical events that result in the beginnings of telepathy and heightened empathy.

The sigil that you created and inscribed on the nanon is its programming and its energy supply, activated by your Magickal charging of the initial image. When the operation's over, record it in your Magickal Record and move on to other things.

Information should be freely available to all. There should be no restriction on ideas. No idea can be unthinkable; no idea is above debate and proof. With the growth of our global communications network, information spreads almost instantaneously. A "telephone tree"—a relatively low-tech method—can spread information continent-wide in less than an hour; computer nets are faster. All information exists eternally in the Akasha; correctly configured consciousness can access it.

A danger of Level 8 is identifying too closely with your ideas. Ideas are designed to carry information; loading them with notions of authority, honor, security, fear, pride, denial, or other baggage will cause them to malfunction. Humans are notoriously scrambled in their Levels 9 and 8. Part of your Initiation in Level 8 consists of disentangling the levels within yourself.

One of the factors contributing to the entanglement is the tide of hormones urging us to mate, to fall in love, to defend our turf, etc.: the survival urges of Level 9. We're good at using mind to rationalize instinct or emotion-driven decisions; we also excel in mistaking impulse for inspiration, feeling for thinking, mind for will.

The traditional symbol for mind is the sword or athame. The mind functions as a blade in analysis, slicing through complexities to find the simplest patterns. Emotions, in part, are reactions to ideas and they condition our processing of ideas. Emotions are native to Levels 10, 9 and 8 simultaneously, in that they have chemical triggers and in that the chemical triggers can be activated by ideas. Ideas and concepts are usually colored by the emotions, even when we think them in a state of calm and peace.

Thinking leaves tracks on MRI screens and EEGs; science says thinking is associated with the firing of neurons in the brain. Thinking is bioelectrical activity that can be detected and measured on Level 10. Thinking discovers the wisdom of instinct, the knowledge of self-perception and the understanding of patterns.

Mind's task is to achieve clarity, patience, and self-knowledge. As part of the Level 8 Initiation, use your Magickal Record to take inventory of yourself and the baggage you might be putting upon your ideas. Take inventory of your ideas, both those you consider original and those from other people.

In the West, there's a myth that the mind rules behavior, that humans are rational animals and that we deserve the name *Homo sapiens*—man, the wise. The mind functions within biological tides and sociopolitical pressures. It's only through honest discipline that you can attain pure thought.

Purity of thought accepts challenges calmly and revises conclusions in the light of new data. Purity of thought prevents you from feeling attacked when your ideas are challenged, or when your mental capacity is called into question. Mind must develop a Zen sensibility for its own function and duty.

Mind provides will with information used in decision- making. Under invocation of Maat, mind labels emotionally biased ideas so will is aware of them. Scanning Level 9 from Level 8, you can see your emotions more clearly and in firmer context. Situations in one level are better seen from a level with less density.

Mind takes pleasure in elegant ideas. Working Magick demands that elegance on all levels for its success. Using the Tree of Life or some other system, mind classifies experiences for fast comparisons, contrasts, and correspondences. Mind, on Level 8, oversees and witnesses information gained on other levels, classifies and correlates it, and readjusts former theories and hypotheses.

Level 8 includes the essence of communication, of twins, of instantaneous information present in both particles, no matter what the distance between them, of Marassa, of the Androgyne/Gynander, of Hermes.

When you approach the Dance of the Mask in the Practice Section, consider that this rite not only provides useful tools, but also exercises your mind's purity of thought. Remember to record this working in your M.R.

NETZACH / VICTORY

THE NEXT LEVEL OF RARITY BEYOND MIND DEALS WITH relationships of all kinds. Your initial experiences in Level 7 should concern your own relationships—with other people, with the environment, with ideas and principles, with the various aspects of yourself. Level 7 is also the world of artistic creativity and inspiration.

In Maat Magick, there are three major areas of practice in Level 7: the invocation of godforms, Sex Magick, and the making of art. Traditionally, invoking means calling a higher intelligence, such as a god, an angel, etc., into your body, your mind, and your soul. You offer yourself to the invoked entity as a vehicle of Level 10 action.

Magickal possession by a godform differs from religious possession in that you remain conscious and share your body with the god form during and after your becoming him/her/it. You are both the god(dess) and yourself; by paying attention to all action under invocation, you learn about the god form in itself and as an aspect of yourself.

In religious possession, the godform supplants the worshipper's consciousness while the worshipper is embraced in timeless ecstasy. Although some memories can remain, often devotees only learn of their body's actions from witnesses.

Like religious invocation, Magickal invocation requires an absolute belief in the godform being summoned, else the invocation is an empty (and dangerous) charade. A problem arises here, since many come to Magick through a shattered faith. How can you believe in a god when you've lost faith in a God who permits evil to afflict the innocent?

Begin by researching the gods of various pantheons through reading and contemplation. Compare and contrast among the pantheons, selecting corresponding gods and determining their shared aspects. You'll find that most of our gods represent the levels of density in their nature, appearance, and deeds.

Level 7 godforms are those of love and creativity: Venus, Aphrodite, Bast, Erzulie, Kama, etc. Level 8 godforms are those of knowledge, science, and communication: Mercury, Hermes, Thoth, Dagon, Hanuman, Coyote, Loki, etc. Level 9 is represented by: Artemis, Diana, Hecate, Khonsu, Chandra, etc., and Level 10 has the earth-god forms of Demeter, Isis, Ceres, Geb, Cernunos, Gaia, etc. Further correspondences can be obtained from 777. Feel free to choose a godform from any level; all are within range of your devotion.

Study the legends of the gods that survive in myth and story. Select a godform that embodies a principle you wish to strengthen in your life. This could be in communications, love, imagination, courage, strength, good judgment, or any number of things. There's some value in selecting a godform that you're not particularly drawn to or even one that repels you; it keeps the process honest.

If you're familiar with the High Tongue of poetry, you know the power of a metaphor to call up an image with fresh connections. Contemplate the principle you wish to incorporate, and how the selected godform represents that principle. Consider the centuries of worship poured into the godform, the nature of offerings made to it. Know that any metaphor or image acquires an independent life of its own and becomes a person of power when enough belief/respect energy is given to him/her/it.

Since the Enlightenment, people who saw God as a sham in the light of science embraced and deified ideas, philosophies and theories, however imperfectly understood. Consider the godlike effects of such abstractions that humans have worshipped, like the divine right of kings, Aryan supremacy, Marx-Leninism, capitalism, evolution, patriotism, etc.

A recent ray of light is the Gaia hypothesis; this abstraction is rooted in observation, and reaches to the prehistoric past for the godform of Gaia, the living Earth as mother of all lives upon her. Science and religion marry here again (much to the annoyance of certain scientists and religionists).

You can acquire belief in a godform through conviction of practice. Do something often enough and long enough, and it will become dense and tangible for you.

Build an altar and shrine for your chosen godform in your temple on Level 10 and on Level 9. Find or create an image of your god form and keep it on the shrine altar. Envision yourself as a devotee, calling and inviting the godform as you would a lover. Decorate the altar and shrine with colors, flowers, metals, herbs, and incenses appropriate to your godform.

Four times a day—sunrise, noon, sunset and midnight—perform your devotions to your godform according to its own proper tradition, or according to ways of your own devising. Whenever possible, work in your temple on Level 10 and Level 9. When circumstances prevent this, work in your Astral Temple. Do a banishment before and after your rite, in any event.

To begin with, you might want to direct the ritual as follows:

—Sunrise: purification and hymns of praise;
—Noon: prayers for boons and blessings, thanks for favors granted;
—Sunset: food offerings and/or communion, offerings of the apt and valuable;
—Midnight: passionate invocation of the godform, silence and stillness of waiting.

Devise an amulet or symbol of your god(dess) that you can wear inconspicuously during the day and safely during the night. Seek out opportunities for performing deeds pleasing to your god(dess). (I recommend that you refrain from Thuggee in the case of Kali worship.)

Think about the god(dess) in the course of the day, and as you fall asleep at night. Open yourself to the mystery of the god(dess); let it enflame your desire for union with him/her. You'll find yourself spontaneously invoking during the rites of sunrise, noon, and sun-

INVOCATION

set. Let it happen. Continue until you experience the indwelling of the god(dess).

Examine your life through the eyes of the god(dess); note what pleases and displeases him/her/you about it. Observe the decisions you make and the actions you perform while being the god(dess), then consider their application, if any, to your normal state of consciousness. Be especially careful about this process when invoking any form of the Trickster, and refrain from doing anything that's fundamentally against your will.

Continue your invocational rituals until you know that you've absorbed the particular godform as thoroughly as possible. Once you've finished your first successful invocation process, choose a few other gods to experience until you're adept at invoking. As your experience grows, you'll be able to invoke any god in a single ritual without the lengthy devotional process, but don't try to cut corners in your initial experiments.

In addition to the benefits of invocation to your own spiritual development, it's useful in your practical Magick. When you design an intentional ritual, include invocation before the decisive symbolic action. Do the major part of the rite as the god(dess), bringing your divine power into the process. Again, the godform invoked should be one whose specialty has a bearing on the situation you're doing Magick to change. As your familiarity with the levels of density grows, your accuracy in picking the right godform for your purpose improves. Check with the table of correspondences in 777 for traditional divine assignments.

In an intentional ritual, it's important that you release your invoked god(dess) before ending the rite and leaving the temple. The reason for this is that you don't want the imbalance of a particular deity in your daily life unless you're in a course of devotional practice. The gods and goddesses are partial, if powerful, entities, competent in their specialties but lacking the full spectrum of the density levels. The universe at large has all the levels, as do human beings, but the gods personify particular principles.

In addition to experiencing the gods personally and adding power to your practical Magick, invocation teaches you the techniques of love under will. Love without will is sentimentality and will without love is tyranny. Love under will can be seen as self-control in the face of overwhelming attraction, but it also means being able to embrace the fearsome, the repulsive or the boring if will requires it.

Love needs belief in its object, even as invocation does. This doesn't mean making excuses for someone you're attached to, or ignoring the true condition of another person; rather, it means you can will yourself to love as you can will yourself to believe. Faith can be useful, in that it aids endurance and survival, but it can be restrictive if it's used as a shelter from spiritual work and individual decisions.

The point is to have both faith and love submissive to will in order to prevent either from running your life. This doesn't mean that will prevents you from falling in love or being drawn to a particular god(dess), but it enables you to see situations clearly and make balanced decisions. There's a powerful physical component in romantic love and religious devotion (and the two are often confused).

The astral bodies of pheromones, hormones, and other secretions power the phenomena of religious devotion, romantic love and artistic creativity. We think our mind or our soul directs our actions and passions; the pursuit of self-knowledge reveals the amazing influence of our physical and astral chemistry on important life decisions. One of the features of initiation is to gain control of our lives despite the chemical barrages we live with.

The key to control is to arouse the astral secretions through acting as if the physical secretions were active. If we meditate on the object/entity we will to love, invoke it four times a day, make offerings to it, and act in ways pleasing to it, we eventually convince all of our bodies to participate in such devotion.

What can be aroused can be dampened, but not by a direct reversal. Hatred isn't the opposite of love since it also involves the concentration of attention on its object. Hatred is the mirror-image of love; love's true enemy is indifference, withdrawal of attention. So it is with faith.

Attention is the hand of will; it can touch lightly, grasp firmly, drop indifferently, strike decisively. It can be attracted, repulsed, diverted, or distracted. Attention relies upon and directs your inner and outer senses, and its natural interests are formed from your survival urges, your character, intelligence, emotions, and tastes.

Initiation includes the establishment of will's control over attention. This is a delicate matter, since you don't want to desensitize yourself and narrow your range of action. On the contrary, will's responsibility to the attention is to train it properly: to lengthen its endurance through the practice of concentration, to widen and deepen it through education and experience, and to refine its subtlety through exploration of the levels of density.

Willed attention is a source of great Magickal power. In order to know another person well enough to assist his or her initiation, you have to pay the coin of attention to what s/he says and leaves unsaid, facial expressions, body language, aura emanations and emotional vibrations. In order to find out what your will is in an ambivalent situation, pay attention to both your strong outer responses and your silent inner directives.

In invocation, sex magick and the creation of art, your attention must be so focused that everything disappears into the event in the process: external surroundings, mental commentary, and self-awareness. You become the event.

Sex magick is a popular topic among Magickians since it combines two major interests in life. The biological event of completed heterosexual intercourse resulting in pregnancy is DNA's prime directive in multicellular life. DNA is a cunning little god, enticing with desire and rewarding with pleasure the individuals and species who obey its directives.

Humans and other vertebrates have discovered ways to avoid the intended results of sex while enjoying the enticements and rewards, consciously or unconsciously. Homosexuality and masturbation, oral and anal sex, contraception and sublimation are all means to this end.

While there are various ways to unencumbered pleasure on Level 10, initiated tradition states that every orgasm produces a child on *some* level of density. The vast majority of nonphysical children inhabit Level 9, on the lower astral planes. The Sex Magickian and initiated artist produce Magickal children of directed and controlled nature, of rarer densities, that manifest in Level 10 in forms other than that of their parent(s).

The Mass of Maat in *Liber Pennae Praenumbra* (see p. 93) is described in the High Tongue of poetry. It combines Eastern and Western Sex Magick principles and technique, and is written in terms of heterosexual coupling. A little ingenuity can adapt it for various gender and number situations.

In prose: the Mass of Maat involves a familiarity with the chakras, major energy complexes in the physical and astral bodies that are aligned vertically along the midline. The chakras correspond with the anus, the genitals, the navel, the heart, the throat, the middle of the forehead, the midpoint on the back of the head, and a few inches above the top of the skull.

The participants must agree on the purpose of the rite, which can be initiatory or practical. They can do it in their normal Magickal personae, with one in godform, or with both in godform. If you choose the latter course, it's best to choose traditional divine couples, like Hadit-Nuit, Shiva-Shakti or Frey-Freya, or adulterous divine couples like Mars-Venus or Ogun-Erzuli. If you invoke deities-as-principles, choose opposite, polarized concepts.

Whatever the polarity arrangement, the substance and material base for manifestation in Sex Magick is the elixir. The elixir is the intentionally charged measure of sexual fluids secreted during the rite. The elixir of Sex Magick's alchemy functions strongly on Levels 10 and 9. When you first charge and then destroy elixir and that which you've charged with it on Level 10, all of its strength is given to its Level 9 (or rarer) body and to the manifestation of your sigilized desire.

You needn't invoke a divine partner, nor the entity of your sigil, in order to perform successful solo Sex Magick.

Both the male semen and female orgasmal fluids are complete sacraments, though of opposite charges. When a man and woman work this higher alchemy together, their natural polarity builds a charge on its own which translates into energy for change when conjoined.

Homosexual and solo workings also involve polarity, but of different natures. Heterosexuality is the attraction of the Other; homosexuality is the attraction of the self in the Other and the Other in the self, as is autosexuality under invocation or in the dream-state. Autosexuality as oneself is the attraction of the self for its transcendence, and of transcendence for the self, through the dissolution of ecstasy. These categories are general and by no means strict divisions. Elements of each accompany the others.

Sex magick can be used for initiation or for practicality, or both simultaneously. There are Eastern practices in sex magick in Tantra, or "Kama Yoga." The Christian approach to sex magick has been almost entirely negative, attempting to deny and defy the sex urge as sinful. Most of the results of this negative approach inhabit the lower astral planes, frustrations balked of satisfaction.

Negative sex magick, or attempted repressions of the urge, arises from a hatred of matter and density. Many Christians, old pagans and some Magickians see Level 10 as disgusting and inferior to the realms of pure spirit. They see matter, particularly the human physical body, as a trap for and a hindrance to spirit, an anchor to a realm of darkness and pain.

There are those who suspend or forego a "normal" sex life so that the energies ascend the chain of the chakras to find their expression in the creation of beauty through art, or in mystic visions. The full physical expression of sex is also helpful to artistic creation; it remains up to you to select the course of action most helpful to your initiation and your art.

Sometimes it's useful to abstain from sexual release during the idea-seeking and image-forming stages, then to practice Sex Magick (precise in timings, intention, and execution) during the Level 10 creation stages. Often, creation of new art happens while the artist is just playing with the materials, instrument, exercises, etc. In this happy event, simply dedicate each spontaneous sexual act to the work in progress and finish your creation.

The point of Sex Magick is to harness one of the most potent forces in life to the service of will. It's a true discipline, requiring more self-control than the abstinence of fear or loathing. In Sex Magick, we recognize the work our DNA has done to ensure its combining and propagating through us. We stand in awe and reverence before the cunning and force of our hard-wiring; the most powerful god in Level 10 with Level 4 configurations is DNA and Sex Magick is the science and the art of directing, aiming and employing its power to cause change in conformity with will.

The strength of sexual attraction in humans is required by the long human childhood. The basic motives of DNA are unaffected by any particular mode of expression, and its strength is undiminished by circumstances in healthy individuals.

At this writing, there is no cure for the plague of AIDS. This disease is debilitating and fatal, and is spread through the exchange of semen or blood. Partnered Sex Magick/alchemy requires the exchanging and blending of one or both of these fluids. It follows, then, that a pair of Sex Magickians engaged in mutual work need to take extraordinary precautions.

Both should be tested for HIV after a six-month period of abstinence from partnered sex. During the period of the agreed-upon alchemy, both partners must abstain from sex with any other person and avoid any other risky behavior that could result in HIV infection.

Occasionally someone tells me that s/he doesn't have to worry about AIDS because s/he is following True Will and therefore the Magickal Current will protect this person from any infection. This is stupid.

The HIV viruses have their own True Will, which is to survive and propagate. There are a lot more of them than there are of us, and unit number strength can be a deciding factor in a contest of wills. If we give HIV an entrance, it will invade. Proper precautions will prevent this.

In current popular parlance, Level 7 represents right-brain activity, Level 8 deals with left-brain activity, and Level 9 concerns the pre-cerebral brain's instincts and urges. Level 6 is the density of post-cerebral integration of the self.

TIPHERETH / BEAUTY

I USED TO INSIST THAT, BEFORE BEGINNING THE PRAC- tice of Maat Magick, a person be established in the Knowledge and Conversation of the Holy Guardian Angel. The process of K & C of HGA (a term used by Aleister Crowley from the *Sacred Magick of Abra Melin the Mage*) is the integration of your identity and the con- sequent discovery of your True Will. This is a process that can take a lot of time and work, or it can be a simple recognition of what you've always known.

Now I've decided to include the primary Initiation of Level 6 in the context of Maat Magick, with a recommendation that you seek out and study Crowley's words on that subject, particularly in *Liber Samekh*.*[1]

The Holy Guardian Angel has been known by other names, such as Daimon, guiding spirit, Higher Self, and so on. Among the symptoms of knowing your HGA and your True Will are a strong sense of purpose, a clear vision of the shape of your work, and a sat- isfaction and joy in the doing of it. Symptoms of not knowing your Angel and your Will are stress and pressure, a sense of directionless drifting and a general malaise of the spirit.

When you begin on the path of initiation, you embark on a search of truth, for Maat. In Levels 10, 9, 8 and 7, you discover

---

[1]*Gems from the Equinox*, Aleister Crowley. Israel Regardie, ed. (Las Vegas: Falcon Press, 1988).

truths about your faculties and abilities. You learn how to use your assets to assist your initiations and your magick. At Level 6, you learn who you are through the faculties trained and activated by your work on the denser levels.

Invoke Maat, that you should know the truth of your own existence. Use the ways of invocation that you learned on Level 7. Sit before a mirror in candlelight, gazing into your own eyes, repeating IPSOS as a mantram (see p. 99). While maintaining focus on your image's eyes, take note of your peripheral vision. What you see in the image of the room behind you could provide you with useful information. Be persistent and invoke at least once a day.

Take inventory of yourself with mental powers you developed on Level 8. What are your desires, inclinations, and talents? Obtain your natal chart; astrology doesn't predetermine your life, but it gives you an idea of what's in your incarnational toolbox. Make an honest search of your memories to review your behavior and feelings in various situations. What do your actions and reactions tell you about yourself?

Examine your dreams—sleeping and waking. What work provides you emotional satisfaction? What do you learn from the images you use in the silent language of dreams? Whom do you admire or disdain, and why? Use your experiences on Level 9 to observe and note your interests.

On Level 10, what sort of work is your body fit to do? How would you rate your strength, agility, endurance, dexterity, speed, and balance? What assets do you have in your family, state of wealth, education, social connections, and reputation? Your work on Level 10 will enable you to better assess yourself here.

In addition to vigorous self-assessment and patient receptivity, you need to clear yourself of distraction in order to meet your HGA. The most serious distractions are difficulties with money, love, and sex, or any clash of wills. When anyone tries to persuade, command, or manipulate you into doing what s/he wants you to, it can be a distraction, but you can use it to observe your own will.

Far more insidious are your own urges, desires, and hormones. Falling in love with the wrong person, being stuck in a bad job, or being in the middle of a job-hunt, or seeking to please a parent or partner, are among the most distracting situations, as are illness and pain. It's difficult to hear your own inner voice while struggling to cope with stressful conditions, but often there's little choice.

Many times, ignorance of your True Will is the factor that induced your distractions in the first place. If you wait until "things clear up" to seek your True Will, you'll wait until hell freezes over. A good banishment is your tool for clearing time and space in which to invoke truth and recognize it.

The revelation of the HGA and True Will can happen as a definite event, accompanied by visions and ecstasy, it can be a silent "click" as your point of view shifts to a wider and deeper perspective, or it can be a gradual dawning in a series of individual revelations. It's helpful to step outside your mind (and the rest of yourself) to watch yourself from an objective distance.

Your HGA has been waiting for you all your life, yearning for you, watching out for you, courting you in a thousand subtle ways. Provide an opening for it and it will rush to embrace you.

A strong method for attaining K & C of HGA is to take a Magickal Oath, under witness of Maat, to continue in your invocation of the HGA until you are united with it. A Magickal Oath is strictly binding and will be manifested in one way or another. There is a purpose to your existence; there are no accidents. Your main obligation in life is to discover your purpose and work on its fulfillment.

Once you comprehend your True Will and begin to work on it, you'll draw people to you without conscious effort. Some will have interest in action congruent with your own, others will diverge, and still others may oppose you. In all cases, you're obliged to help each one's spiritual evolution, according to individual need. This does not mean that you should do other people's work, or even imply that you could. The most you need to do is teach by example, suggest reading material, and raise as many questions as you answer.

You'll know your HGA by the clarity of purpose that it brings, and by a fresh view of life in which many puzzling factors fall into place and make sense to you. Be sure that you're firmly established in your new state of being before beginning the next stage of your Level 6 work.

MEETING THE ANGEL

The next stage is a return to Level 9 and your Astral Temple for the invocation of the Forgotten Ones. These are entities of the astral planes that are rooted in the pre-cerebral brain; they are the survival urges that have been layered over by the higher functions of intellect and logic. The Forgotten Ones include, but are not limited to, the instincts of hunger, sex, fight-or-flight, clanning, communication, curiosity, altruism and religion, all those imperatives of actions ensuring survival of self, offspring, and species.

The gods our ancestors worshipped are rooted in the Forgotten Ones, given typical human personalities, then made larger and more powerful than humans. We create our gods in our image and likeness. The process of creating gods arises from our self's need to rationalize its instinctive behavior to itself, and to seek protection from natural events that threaten the survival of the self, offspring, and species.

The gods and goddesses of the old pantheons gained independent life through centuries of worship and did play a directing role in the spiritual, moral and social lives of their devotees. The ancient divinities hold a residual power that is being reanimated by contemporary Neopagans and Magickians in new and different ways.

The monotheism of Judaism, Christianity and Islam effectively cut off the energy of public worship and belief from the pagan pantheons. These major world religions represent an early attempt to transcend the anthropomorphism of the pagan gods and reach for a more abstract understanding of deity. The concept of an historical Christ won the Petrine/Pauline conflict; with the popular and official defeat of the Gnostic Christ in the early Church, divinity was once more couched in human terms.

The Ancient Egyptians had de-emphasized the human aspects of their divinities by giving them animal heads or symbolic crowns and calling them *neter* or principles. Pharaoh Akhenaten promoted monotheism during his reign, but the idea died with him. Some Neopagans realize their chosen pantheons are symbols of various principles, although others persist in the usual personifications.

In order to attain the next step in the continuum of perspectives on divinity, it's necessary to draw the bowstring of comprehension back to an intimate acquaintance with the Forgotten Ones, upon whom the religious impulse and attraction to mystical experience are founded.

I strongly advise that you do not attempt an invocation of the Forgotten Ones until you are firmly established in Level 6 and its revelations of your true identity. Not until you become familiar with your own divine essence should you call up your survival urges/Forgotten Ones/ "demons" to conscious awareness and integration with your true self.

The Forgotten Ones are not only stronger than one would think, but they are also the roots of demons and devils as well as the roots of gods.

In the traditional Abra Melin Operation, after invoking your Angel, you are supposed to evoke and bind the demons to do your bidding. So it is in Maat Magick, but with a comprehension of the metaphors of the literal actions. The Invocation of the Forgotten Ones is in the Practice Section of this book.

Many traditions of mysticism speak of the need to discipline and chastise the body in order to conquer the animal desires and free the attention for spiritual development. This notion is usually part of the view that matter is bad and spirit is good, matter is dirty and spirit is pure, matter is illusion and spirit is reality. Those who hold this opinion are barred from understanding themselves and the Cosmos by the unquestioned assumption that an opposing dualism is the essence of reality.

The survival urges are hard-wired behavior directives encoded in our DNA. They enabled our ancestors to survive long enough to develop a conscious intelligence. This intelligence is still in its juvenile/naive stage, in which it's embarrassed by the survival urges and tries to overcome, glorify, externalize, or deny them. We've split our inner view of them in complexities of religion and myth.

On the side of "Light," we've deified our behaviors and their Forgotten Ones as gods, God, and divine incarnations. We draw abstract qualities from observed behaviors and name those qualities virtues and sins. With the invocations of Level 7, we've experienced the divine aspects of our behavioral guides.

On the side of "Darkness," we encounter the blindness and strength of the Forgotten Ones, the terrible and terrifying results of their being misdirected through wrong ideas and warped emotions.

Beyond the individual's and the species' DNA patterns, the Forgotten Ones link with forces "outside" our individuality, cosmic forces and forms that share with us a participation in the Universal Pattern of Consciousness, and thus share a mutual interaction with us. The religious urge in humanity should be considered a Forgotten One, itself.

Discussion is no substitute for direct experience.

I've found that the invocation of the Forgotten Ones is effective for calling them up in myself, experiencing them, becoming them, and integrating them consciously into my life and Magickal Work. The Forgotten Ones can obsess the unbalanced and come to dominate their lives, providing access for their linked cosmic forces and forms to enter the shared realities of humanity in disastrous ways. One thinks of Hitler, Stalin, Vlad the Impaler, Caligula, Nero, etc., in this regard. This is why it's important that you are balanced in your Higher Self before attempting this type of Working.

When you have reached the proper balance in Level 6, however, you need to integrate the Forgotten Ones as part of your initiation since they are power sources, are means of earthing your Magick, and are necessary to your understanding of yourself, other people and situations.

Each succeeding initiation into rarity is important. It sometimes happens that they're not experienced in strict order; some levels are leapt over in sudden revelation of levels beyond. Sooner or later, levels that were flown over have to be walked through.

The final task of Level 6 should be a consolidation of all denser levels into your integrated self, particularly the ones skipped over, if any. The essence of Level 6 is beauty. At Level 6, you become an adept, an effective Magickian who must walk in beauty. Balance and harmony are beauty's friends, as is the rightness of doing True Will.

GEBURAH / STRENGTH

LEVEL 5 IS, TRADITIONALLY, THE DENSITY OF STRENGTH in its martial form. In Maat Magick, strength is acquired in subtle ways not always attributable to Mars. Your balanced and integrated self in Level 6 has the strength inherent in balance and integration. Exploration of the rarer densities requires strengths of different types and intensities beyond that which you need for daily living. The further you progress along the way of initiation, the more diffi-cult becomes the path.

The first aspect of strength is endurance, the ability to perse-vere in your work despite weariness and fatigue, challenge and oppo-sition. The sensible course of acquiring endurance includes planning your times for rest and sleep and practicing methods of relaxation and stress release. Make a daily practice of Hatha Yoga, meditation or pranayama. Physical exercise is important, as are housekeeping chores done well.

Endurance grows in the practice of itself. At the density of 5, you practice it on your current life and work. In some cases, en-durance means remaining in unpleasant, painful, or dangerous cir-cumstances in order to accomplish something important to your True Will.

Such circumstances can surround you suddenly or gradually; your endurance in either case is measured by necessity and is there-fore limited. Nothing lasts forever; you need to sustain your partici-pation only long enough to make the proper changes. In some situations, these changes are within yourself; in others, the changes are in other people, natural physical conditions, or in the right alignment of influences.

You are the only thing upon which you can work directly. You cannot force another person to change, but you can present opportunities and information that would be helpful. Part of endurance is the wisdom to recognize hopeless cases and to know when to quit.

There are occasions for endurance where quitting isn't an option, such as a prison sentence, responsibility for the care of children or the elderly, or personal disability. Even here, time brings an end to the situation by service, maturity, or death. Initiatory practices can be modified to fit conditions by using the freedom of your mind plus a little ingenuity.

Another aspect of strength is invisibility. In many communities, the practice of Magick is regarded as Satanism and anything occult is automatically considered evil. It's usually a bad idea to taunt troublemakers or to make a political statement by cultivating a spooky image—unless, of course, it's part of a more comprehensive scheme.

In most situations, it's wise to blend in with your surroundings, to adopt a type of protective coloration with your image, so you can pursue your work with minimal distractions. Dancing the Mask of normalcy renders you invisible.

One of the inbuilt rites of passage in life is the identification with one's own generation in adolescence. Secret languages are invented, new popular music emerges and the contemporaries' tribal customs of dress, grooming and behavior are chosen to distinguish the young from their parents.

The Neopagan community is a diverse group of people of various trades and backgrounds. The annual gatherings and festivals are wonderful occasions for self-expression through one's costume (or lack of any). 'Tis far better to save your special garb for such occasions than to wear black and bedeck yourself with pentagrams amid the general public.

Should your Magick lead you into danger on the physical plane—where the danger resides in other people's probable reactions and actions—use your wits and invention.

On the inner, invisibility is also a form of strength, especially if you feel opposition to your work or if you feel under psychic attack. Envisioning your aura as a diamond-hard shield surrounding you usually is sufficient to make yourself invisible from Level 9 on up. When you're invisible in this fashion, you become less visible on Level 10.

In creating an effect, or in manifesting will, an invisible hand strengthens the work. Making your art strong enough to stand on its own often requires your disappearing into your art as you craft it. The less your personality intrudes into your art, the more universal that art becomes. As your art becomes more universal, it acquires the strength to penetrate and subvert the most adamant of personal censors in your audience's minds.

Universality doesn't mean that your characteristic touches in style, manner or flavor sink into vapid anonymity. On the contrary: keeping your ego and personality out of the creation of art permits your true hand to express universals in its unique way. Trust in the wisdom of your true hand directed by True Will.

A third aspect of strength is power, the ability to manifest your will through appropriate means. Here again, the basic principle is to become transparent (invisible) to the Magickal Current, impressing upon it the signal of your will as the carrier wave of the current passes through you.

The more precisely you align yourself with Tao, with the ongoingness of things, the more power becomes available to you. In order to achieve such alignment, you must observe the world around you in order to comprehend the nature of the flow that moves behind it.

Strength gives birth to courage. Conversely, successfully met challenges to courage confirm you in greater strength. I suggest an exercise that I did for Level 5: camp out overnight alone.

Pick your location according to its degree of isolation and innate power. I drove from Cincinnati to the Red River Gorge in the Daniel Boone Park forest in Kentucky. It was October, clear and cold. I fashioned a lean-to from a blanket and branches, built a fire before it and positioned my sleeping bag beneath it.

After drumming the sun to rest and invoking Maat, I lay down in the sleeping bag and watched the stars appear. In the absence of

CAMPING OUT

any light-pollution, the Milky Way was clear and deep, and many more stars were visible than I'd ever seen. I felt like I was falling up into the stars; soon after, I experienced the most profound terror that I've ever known. The idea of packing up camp and driving home was out of the question; this was to be an overnight working, and a second chance or opportunity would be a long time coming.

There were animal noises from the woods surrounding the meadow my camp was in, but I sensed no real threat from animals. There were no footfalls nor motor noise to be heard, so I didn't fear human intrusion. The terror came from the solitude of the situation and from the immensity of the star-filled sky.

There seemed to be but one course of action available to me, so I opened myself to the terror, and allowed the stars to draw me from my body and pull me into the sky.

There followed a series of visions of various "aliens" and personified concepts, plus a plunge into the star-thick heart of the Andromeda galaxy. When dawn came, there was frost on the meadow grass and on my sleeping bag.

After I fed the fire's coals to heat the coffee, I checked the ritual site of the previous evening, and the spot where I'd buried a stone talisman. The talisman was gone, and its black velvet wrappings were strewn on the ground around the hole beneath the fallen log where I'd buried it.

The world could be considered a more dangerous place today, eighteen years later, but I think not. The nature of the dangers may change, but life is poised on the brink of death at all times, as it has been from the beginning. The more distracted we are by the minutiae of living, the less aware we are of the annihilating gulf surrounding us. In solitary situations—be it wilderness camping, flotation tanks, cemeteries, etc., the distractions are gone and reality stands unveiled.

We are each a unique individual, with perceptions, thoughts and dreams private to ourselves. We are also social beings, used to the presence and group aura of our fellow humans, or at least our fellow animals. We need psychic contact to thrive and survive; we count as dire punishment solitary confinement or the isolation of being "sent to Coventry," or shunning.

The next stage of humanity's development consists of a strengthening and alignment of the individual's connection to the rest of our species. Our present vague awareness of other people is sharpened and extended to the degree of a second consciousness. One is empathically and telepathically linked to everyone else on the planet.

Our mental input filter prevents an overload, and only by focusing attention on someone can we pick up actual thoughts. Strong emotions and feelings, such as pain and despair, are broadcast with the intensity of personal experience, however, and so we all are careful about each other's well-being.

Maat Magick liberates your time-binding capacity; you can enjoy the benefits of our "future" double consciousness now. You can link with the auras of the entire species and the power inherent in them, and apply this collective power to the working of your will. This rapport extends beyond humanity, with practice, to embrace the cosmos and the chaos around and within it.

Maat's operational title in Level 5 is "Air, the Unconfined." Strength, in all its aspects, becomes yours to the extent you transcend all that confines you. The most important restriction/confinement to overcome is your present notion of yourself.

The discovery of True Will in Level 6 doesn't mark the end of your transformation. Within each level you'll create/encounter one or more new selves. From one point of view, you're just uncovering parts of yourself that you've been unaware of. From another point of view, the initiation process leads you to create new aspects of yourself as you achieve greater levels of rarity. I tend to side with the second view, from personal experience.

Among other things it does to and for us, the little god DNA winds our clocks and sets our time. It determines the lengths of our stages and appoints the times of our passage in the sequence of zygote-blastula-embryo-fetus-infant-toddler-child-adolescent-parent-senior-corpse. Each stage has its proper initiatory work, its benefits useful to comprehending a particular level of density.

When you experience an enlightening event that pertains to your current stage of maturity and you are free from hindering encumbrances, the key turns in the lock and the door swings open upon a new way of seeing things. When you use the assets available to you according to your new way of seeing, you build a new aspect of yourself.

Part of initiatory transformation is gaining a wider context of reality and a more comprehensive perspective of your concerns, your cosmic/chaotic function, and your place in the food chain.

As you achieve new levels of rarity, you can return to operate on denser levels when appropriate. You bring your larger, more rarified viewpoint with you when you do so; you won't duplicate your former state of consciousness, but you'll enjoy a more sophisticated appreciation of the denser levels.

Traditionally, Level 5 is a narrowing, a concentration of force in the fashion of a laser. This is applicable in Maat Magick in the solitary "vision quest" exercise mentioned previously. To enter Level 4, it's necessary to expand. There is an expansion method in the Practice Section.

CHESED / MERCY

IN DENSITY LEVEL 4, YOU BRING YOUR INITIATED SELF to the fullness of its nature. The course of your initiation has seen you enlightened, rebalanced, and established in your physical body and its environment, in the realm of dreams, instincts and imagings, in the intellect, in your relationships with other people and nature in general, your union with your Holy Guardian Angel and the discovery of your True Will, in your strength and endurance. One of your tasks in the fourth rarity is to coordinate all of these into your initiated individuality and set them into harmonious action.

The other tasks of this level include awakening your Kundalini, or serpent-power, to its full extent, and writing your thesis of the universe and your plans for improving it.

Kundalini is a Hindu concept that has a great value in Magick as a tool for achieving your full potential as an agent for change and as a human being. Kundalini is pictured as a serpent of force that lies coiled three-and-a-half times at the base of the spine. It's intimately related to the major chakras, in that the serpent-force both activates each chakra as it rises in its spinal channel, and is drawn upward by the activation of each chakra.

Kundalini's major channel of ascent is called the Sushumna, which is flanked on either side by the Ida on the left and the Pingala on the right. These side channels are connected to the nostrils, and their balance, which ensures the balance of the Sushumna, is best established by the practice of pranayama, or Yogic breathing. (See Practice Section, Level 4.) Pranayama is a purifying, as well as a balancing, practice; when the purification is complete, Kundalini will rise on its own. Sometimes Kundalini rises on its own, with no conscious effort of preparation; imaged meditation, as in Crowley's *Liber HHH*, also works. We'll discuss this more fully in the Practice Section.

Before you can improve the universe, you must accurately assess its present condition and identify problems. Even though we fascinate ourselves inordinately, any honest survey of our surroundings shows that human beings, singly and in various combinations, are both source and ultimate victims of all problems and wrongs to be righted. The rest of Nature is innocent and perfect, unless there are races elsewhere in conditions similar to our own.

The notion of improving the universe is tied to the striving for personal perfection natural to Level 4. If you've done your work properly on the denser levels, you begin another process of integration, similar to that of Level 6, but in a more comprehensive way, on a vaster scale. Your powers of visualizing and imaging are more precise and far-ranging. Your charisma that you ignited in Level 6 radiates strongly enough to influence everyone you meet.

You recognize the boundaries of your individuality and probable lifespan. You understand your limits of time and energy and their relationship to the magnitude of your chosen task. You comprehend the Magickal machinery necessary to link your personal assets and intentions with the Magickal Current/ongoingness of things/Tao, and then to the work of change at hand.

In Level 4, you traverse the scale of existence, from minute to vast, monadic simplicity to fractal complexity. In each level of density, there are the aspects of inner and outer, the search for truth and its practical applications. Our consciousness sits at the gate between the inner and the outer, peering, Janus-like, at the workings of the soul, the imagination, and the passions on one hand, and at the unfolding of the material universe through the dimension of time on the other.

I find a delight in the fact that we humans, with the use of instruments of observation, find ourselves in the middle of the range of physical size in the observable universe. We are to subatomic particles what galactic clusters are to us. Meditation on this produces a factor important to personal balance: humility.

Magickal humility is the accurate assessment of your strengths and weaknesses, virtues and vices, prides and shames, and general usefulness to the universe. Magickal humility is not self-abasement, low self-esteem or a claim of helplessness. Religious humility, on the other hand, is "bending the knee" to God, declaring oneself to be an abject sinner in need of divine salvation, an unworthy wretch deserving of damnation.

This attitude isn't acceptable in Magick; you alone are responsible for your soul and your salvation. (For those interested in the Gnostic Christ, read the works of Gerald Massey.) While there are beings with greater abilities than ours on various Levels, we do not trade autonomy for advice, nor responsibility for redemption. Maat Magick is Thelemic Magick; "thou hast no right but to do thy Will."

At the same time, among beings of different abilities, ethics permit us to exchange information and ideas, develop friendships and business deals, trade favors and occasionally fall in love. As you might treat a client or a benefactor to dinner as a matter of etiquette, you can provide energy feasts for your ancestors, gods or Loa.

As for the question of the existence of God and its ramifications, I leave that to you. My own experiences lead to the certainty of a Divine Intelligence inherent in all things. It manifests itself in the way things are, in the way things change, and in the way we comprehend both.

Your moral code as a Maat Magickian is the strictest possible course of awareness and behavior. Your heart must equal Maat's feather in the balance scale in all actions, while you measure as Anubis, record as Tehuti, judge as Osiris, advise as Isis and Nepthys, and devour as Sebekh.

Pledging your consecration to truth opens you to a terrible honesty and awareness. Tales of heaven and hell pale in the light of self-knowledge, where you are certain of the pain you've caused and the damage done. Forgiveness is a self-given gift that dies in false sorrow. Level 4 is traditionally known as Mercy, even though its Jupiter-nature includes judgment of ideas and motives, and justice for deeds.

Magickal humility, when practiced assiduously, orders your actions in conformity with will and love. The meditation which I call the Cosmic Vision can be helpful in judging your importance in the scheme of things. (See Practice Section.)

As a self-aware intelligence, you can find in yourself all the virtues and vices of our species in potential. Which of these you've activated and which you've kept dormant reflect your character and personality. In each of us is a resonance by which we identify with heroes and villains, saints and sinners, the full range of human action from the beautiful deed to the hideous.

All other inhabitants of our planet are essentially innocent in their inability to make moral judgments about their own actions. Our species alone stands in need of improvement. This narrows the field, somewhat, of possible improvements in your plans, though it places no restrictions on your thesis.

A Magickian is a talisman for the rest of the species; what we do to attain higher states of awareness and action directly inspires everyone else who shares our genetic makeup, for good or ill.

In order to formulate your thesis of the universe and your plans for improving it, you need to seek out enough information, outer and inner, upon which to base your conclusions. Read what you can of history, remembering that the winners wrote the books; keep informed of current news, and open yourself to Akashic information.

All time exists simultaneously; we see distant galaxies by very old light. In like manner, the light and sound of a younger Earth and its inhabitants trail our planet like the shedding of a snake. Our temporal skin spirals and twists behind us along the path of our orbit around our sun which is traveling its own course around the galactic center, which is also moving.

It's a dizzy ride, but the astral body's senses are able to perceive our ghostly trace and follow it with the speed of thought to any particular time and place. This ability is guided by the racial memory encoded in our DNA. History books are somewhat helpful for identifying times and people, but trust your own observations.

The fifth-level vortex acts both as a temporal anchor for your travels and as a power source to speed your going and aid your Magick in other times.

While it's true that Magick begins and ends in Level 10, it travels all the levels between ten and one in its course. Your experiences on the various levels will teach you how best to work Magick in each one. The vortex can be focused on or by the level of your choice.

The future is a different proposition. The events of the past have a type of solidity about them, while future events are chaotic. This chaos of the future is not an amorphous soup, but a sheaf of possibilities and probabilities of various degrees of likelihood. Your vortex can afford you the vision of what I call the Probability Universe.

I see it as a combination of fractal froth and tinkertoys, extending round me beyond the limits of sight. As my instant of consciousness moves along its course in this curly maze, it creates a glowing strand. My contemporaries weave their glowing strands with mine until there's a self-illumined fuzzy cable that wanders from node to node.

The nodes represent survival decisions in times of crises and impart to our history its characteristic shape. Our human cable weaves in and out of the cables of other species, plant, animal, microbe and virus that form the web of life on Earth. The Earth—that is, the geosphere, hydrosphere, and atmosphere—weaves the base/background for the cables of the fastlife species.

Behind me glows the terrestial line of mainstream reality. Fanning out from every node are countless if-worlds, worlds of the paths not taken. It's possible to visit them astrally, also.

Before me lie the probability-worlds, also fanning out from future choice-nodes. Whatever collective choices we make, as a species, will be the major guides for our course of mainstream reality. As of this writing, we are in the process of working through such a choice-node.

This node began forming about the time of World War I, acquired the heft and bulk of danger in the growth of the military-industrial complex, became a crisis-node with the development of nuclear weapons and power plants and has begun a hopeful resolution with the collapse of Soviet Communism and the end of the Cold War.

Our present node, like most of the others our species has traversed, accumulated around population growth world-wide. Remov-

N'ATON

ing the tensions of Superpower contention was helpful in liberating more time and attention for the underlying situations.

Maat Magick developed, in part, from the vision of the probability worlds and communion with our future species-self who calls itself N'Aton. The image I have of N'Aton is an androgynous human, strongly lit from the left, the right side in deep shadow in which various sub-images appear. S/He puts me in mind of James Michener's "Golden Man" in *Hawaii*, a handsome and intelligent blend of Polynesian, Oriental, Black, and Caucasian.

I met N'Aton in late 1973 during a time-travel working with a group of Cincinnati Magickians. The core vision s/he shared with me is recorded in *Liber Pennae Praenumbra*. S/He also introduced me to the probability-worlds, pointing out the likely futures fanning out from our present crisis-node.

N'Aton's actuality base lies along one of the fanned-out futures. I also saw some of the alternatives: Earths that were a radioactive cinder, or a ball of sterile sludge, or a withered home to totalitarian regimentation, or a recovering humanless planet, etc.

In N'Aton's home line, we've controlled our mutation into a species of double consciousness: the familiar one of individuality and the new telepathic connection among us that constitutes N'Aton. If one hungers, all feel it; victims and villains share such intimacy that all pain given is simultaneously felt by the giver. If a mind turns to madness, it's comforted and returned to health by everyone around it.

Loneliness and defeat require conscious effort to achieve. Great ideas and insights are easily shared, but not to the detriment of the arts; individual work is cherished and prized.

I leave it to you to extrapolate the socioeconomic effects of double consciousness on our species and our planet. The direct linkage of minds in awareness creates an intelligence larger than our individual brains are capable of supporting.

Current evolutionary theories include the idea that the present form of cells resulted from the symbiotic inclusion of free-living viruses into a permanent home in the cytoplasm. The guest inclusions, such as the mitochondria, perform vital services in chemical production for the cell as a whole.

Our bodies are made of specialized cells cooperating as tissues, organs, and systems. The amazing intelligence of the cell is simpler by an order of magnitude, in terms of complexity and ability, than the intelligence found in multicellular beings. Consider the next order of magnitude of intelligence of an entity who has us as cells: this is N'Aton. The birth of N'Aton marks our debut into interstellar society, since its degree of complexity and integration is the mark of a species' maturity.

Maat Magick aims to accelerate our development into N'Aton since we need that level of intelligence to survive and to reverse the damage we've done to the Earth. It seems to be working, so far. My colleagues and I began working the changes of Maat Magick in 1974.

Several developments indicate to me the beginning of success: the Cold War collapsed along with the Soviet Union and its version of socialism-communism; the development of more effective methods of contraception; the rise of ecological awareness and activism worldwide; feminism's raising the consciousness of the general public; the advances in genetics, communications and computer technology, chaos theory, artificial intelligence research, etc. I've also noticed that the children I've met who were born since the mid-70s seem to be more intelligent, sensitive and aware than formerly.

The process needs close attention and adjustment, however, plus encouragement of new facets of increased racial intelligence as they appear. There's also a need of balancing this emerging double consciousness through the global socioeconomic upheavals that are just beginning.

This vision of probability-worlds, of N'Aton and of the Magickian's power and responsibility to influence the course of mainstream reality underlies the whole of Maat Magick. It's been my blessing to hear from a number of people who share this vision and who recognized their own experiences in the account of my own.

Level 4's initiation and task for you is to discover your own view of the cosmos and your plans for improving it. I share with you my own discoveries in the hope that they can be helpful to your quest.

The N'Aton mutation differs from previous evolutionary leaps in that an individual can achieve double consciousness here and now through personal work.

In a necessarily crude and imperfect way: you achieve the required depth and breadth of awareness by climbing the Tree successfully; you assist others to do the same by descending the Tree bearing your knowledge which you communicate by example, by discourse and by art and Magick of various types.

In the process, you acquire self-knowledge beyond your individuality. You've learned that you aren't circumscribed by your skin or your skull, that your True Self is coterminous with the cosmos. You become more sensitive to the motives and intentions of other people; in recognizing in them that which you've experienced in your individuality, you develop a psychic surety.

This psychic surety often manifests initially in divinations. Many times when I do a tarot reading for someone, the cards serve as a springboard for direct perceptions of the querent's situation. I've heard others tell of similar experiences.

The direct perception happens as an instant rapport with the other person, be it friend or stranger. When you speak to him or her, it's akin to channeling visionary material. You speak with confidence from no evidence, from an unlearned knowledge, and the other person confirms your accuracy.

You can use your favorite divinatory method to extend your psychic surety and rapport to increasingly wider and deeper ranges. Use the same degree of attention, concentration, and awareness that you use for individual divination and gradually expand it.

Do readings on people you know without their being present and check your results in casual conversations. Do readings on public figures and monitor the media for confirming or disproving news. Extend this to groups, corporations, political parties, and nations.

You'll find that your successes mirror your interests at first, but by deliberately focusing your attention, you'll find that you can generate a real interest in anyone or any group.

There are other methods of development of the second consciousness, such as meditation and contemplation, the Martial Arts and Yoga, plus ways you develop on your own.

When unlearned knowledge and unprompted emotions about other people begin to come to you without your seeking, then you've begun to function in double consciousness. This comes in flashes, erratic and sporadic at first, but gaining in consistency and continuity as time goes on.

Your individuality will learn to devise shielding by concentrating on the work at hand and tuning out at will, keeping your new awareness to a manageable background presence. Like any other faculty, the second consciousness improves with use and practice.

By the time you've attained Level 4, you'll have developed a sense of discretion. This sense should tell you to keep your new abilities to yourself. A little thought on human nature reveals that we have a tendency to attack what we don't understand, especially anything that penetrates our identity's perceived sovereignty.

If you speak of the second consciousness, you won't be believed; if you demonstrate it, you won't be trusted. Simply use it as an advantage in the Great Work. Spread the net of your awareness around the planet and learn of conditions firsthand. Read the mood and concerns of anyone, and achieve a sure life with minimal conflict. Anticipate and forestall human problems; become aware of another's readiness for initiation. Through the second consciousness, you'll recognize other mutants and join forces for more efficient work.

Gaining the second consciousness creates for you a moral abyss: do you have the purity of will to refrain from using it unethically? It's possible to fall into sin/self-destruction at any level.

Maat's ethics in the double consciousness during this transitional period forbid its use to gain advantage for yourself in trivial matters or to interfere with another person's True Will. Trivial matters include the pursuit of wealth, status, fame, sex, or control of others. The whole point of Maat Magick is to speed our species' change from *Homo sapiens* to *Homo veritas*.

Those who violate ethics should be mindful that there are other people who participate in the second consciousness. These people see to it that the transition remains clean and free; violations are corrected but the violators wed themselves to the chains of Ego.

This is a drastic unfitting for the next stage of experience, the Abyss.

THE ABYSS

IN THEORY, BY THE TIME YOU'VE ESTABLISHED YOUR mastery of Levels 10 through 4, you've attained perfection. "Perfection" is a relative term, of course, and I'm using it loosely. By it, I mean that if you have developed each aspect of yourself to the point of competence, familiarity and ease, you have balanced the aspects to best promote the manifesting of True Will, and harmlessly accomplish change in conformity with that Will, then you are perfect.

Perfection is relative in the time-dimension also; an infant may be a perfect infant, but only growth and development through time will bring it to perfections of childhood, youth, maturity, and age. The same sliding scale of perfections applies to the Path of Initiation; each level has its phases of introduction, work, and comprehension.

Level 4's perfection marks the boundary of individual initiation, and that of N'Aton as a collective intelligence. Initiation continues, but individual identity and collective identity do not. There are three more levels of rarity to attain, but they lie beyond the realm of duality, beyond your faith in your own reality.

There's a useful analogy to the last three levels of rarity in the field of science. Some descriptions of the subparticle realm convey the image of the energy spectrum developing eddies within itself, generating interference patterns, the nodes of which behave as quarks. The tendency toward complexity in matter draws quarks into particles, particles into atoms, atoms into molecules, molecules into states that are further elaborated, united, consolidated, and changed.

This process reflects the levels of rarity and density, both directly and in reverse. Directly, the consolidation of simplicities into complexities brings an increase of manifested intelligence. In the simpler, more rarified levels of existence, intelligence manifests as trends and tendencies that are named forces: the strong force, the weak force, electromagnetic force and gravitation. These forces encourage unions of parts into wholes, disintegrations, alignments, and attainment of equilibria.

With further infusions of energy, simple matter develops unstable atoms, longchain molecules and the ability of organization and replication, as in crystals and cytoplasm. Intelligence begins to manifest tropism, mobility, hunger and self-preservation in the behavior of single-celled organisms.

As single cells join in cooperative colonies (algae, coral, slime molds), simple plants and animals (lichen, hydra) and in many kinds of life in the Terran biosphere (molluscs, fish, insects, mammals) the breadth and depth of intelligence grows and manifests in instinct, memory, learning, and self-awareness. The increasing complexity of the animal kingdom concentrates in the development of nervous systems and brains. The more neural cells present and the more connections existing among them, the stronger and more layered is the intelligence that can manifest.

Twentieth century humanity works on expanding our body of knowledge and squeezing convenient technology from that expansion. We still ponder the same Big Questions that concerned the ancient Greeks, Egyptians, Sumerians, henge builders, and cave painters. Who am I? What is death? What is the purpose of life? How did we originate and what is our destiny? Why is there evil?

When the manifestation of intelligence reaches the complexity required for self-questioning and reflection, it's ready for a return to its origins. This return is effected by going forward, rather than retracing history.

The progress through the levels of density and rarity described in these pages mark the first stages of our journey homeward. Levels 10 to 4 are basic categories of flesh-linked experiences of individuality or collectivity. The double consciousness of N'Aton is an organization of complexity beyond that of individual consciousness. It loosens the boundaries of experience and broadens our point of view, but remains in the realm of duality.

Levels 3 through 1 are like the energy spectrum before it begins to solidify into matter, before it acquires mass, before its velocity plummets to a level slower than the speed of light. The gap between faster-than-light and sublight velocities is like the Abyss.

Duality is the condition of the material universe and the way we experience it as individuals. The oriental symbol of the yin-yang expresses the inseparability of the "pairs of opposites" in nature: matter-energy, space-time, dark-light, male-female, past-future, death-life, etc. In order to experience the three rarest levels (traditionally termed the Supernals), we must transcend duality in our view and comprehension of reality.

A good preliminary practice is the *neti-neti* meditation, which challenges you to find your essential Self. The only rule is: that which you possess is not your Self. Anything that can be expressed after the word "my" is not you. The list is long, but not infinite. My body or any of its parts, my actions, my feelings and emotions, my mind, my love, my soul, my strength, my visions—none of these are me.

The *neti-neti* can be compared to peeling away the layers of a hollow onion; sooner or later you reach the Nothing at the center. In simply reading these words or thinking about them, you can muster intellectual agreement; only by personal experience will you be able to transcend duality, to cross the Abyss. Unconfirmed by experience, the idea that our essential identity is nothing is the ultimate threat to the combined layers of our hollow onion individuality, or Ego.

Herein lies the danger of the Abyss.

A lifetime of mistaken interpretation of experience lends an unholy strength to the persistence of error. Our unquestioned acceptance of appearances has convinced us that our collection of idiosyncracies and quirks, a collection upon which we hang our name, constitutes an indivisible unit of reality.

The notion of identity resides in a field projected by the cohesion of our parts, a unique combination of influences and sub-pattern variations of the Universal Pattern of Consciousness. The mind and the brain shape each other during life to generate a self that outlives the body, but even that self is hollow at the center.

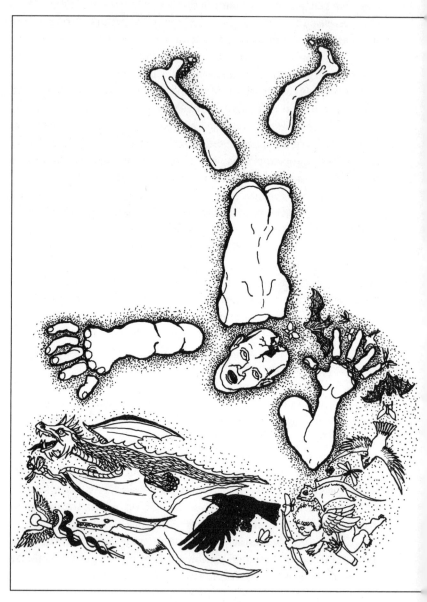

THE ABYSS

When we see a glimpse of the nothing at the heart of the soul, the instinct of self-preservation can trigger profound fear and denial. This fear can inspire people to cling to the existence of Ego, to attempt to hoard and wall up all our parts, aspects, knowledge, and power.

The crossing of the Abyss requires embracing the nothing, letting go of all certainty and conviction, and voluntarily dissolving.

If you've developed and balanced your densities from Levels 10 through 4, they'll continue to operate properly as your outer life requires. Any duties and obligations will be met and fulfilled, any emergencies will be dealt with. It's a good idea to arrange for simpler living during your dealings with the Abyss, if possible. At a minimum, reserve a daily span of time to spend in temple alone.

As you dissolve into your central nothingness, you comprehend that the image of the hollow onion, the hollow sphere is only a snapshot of your configuration. In function, your layers of density form a hollow tube, a channel of force and fire from the rare to the dense, a conduit for Tao.

Here lies the doom of those who would prevent their dissolution into nothing, who would cling to and grasp their levels of density in the vain hope that doing so would preserve themselves in their identity. The influx of force from above the Abyss flows through us, vitalizing our illusions and play in the world. Denying the nothing of our core denies the flow and turns us into a sealed vessel feeding on our own frail substance.

Crowley terms such sealed ones "Black Brothers."

A Black Brother (of any gender), having denied his or her essential nothingness, attempts to find sustenance and life force as a vampire and parasite. There's a contemporary folk-saying that describes a Black Brother: "A man wrapped up in himself makes a mighty small package." Not only is the package small, it dwindles and shrinks as it consumes its own substance, bound for the useless entropy/heat-death of a closed system.

The path of initiation produces failures as well as successes, and a Black Brother is the worst of the failures. In the fury of despair, the Black Brother seeks to fasten upon seekers working through the denser levels, or upon innocent uninitiates, to the end of siphoning life and energy from them. In her book, *Psychic Self*

Defense, Dion Fortune provides methods for handling such a psychic vampire.

For those who accept the central nothingness, Crowley uses the term "Babe of the Abyss." In a type of reverse gestation, your Levels from 9 through 4 deconstruct themselves into spiritual dust. Your 10th Level continues its business in the world, functioning on its memory of perfection and the guidance of True Will.

In the Abyss, silence prevails and time has no meaning. As the 10th Level measures things, one can be in the abyss for days, months or years, being nothing.

Eventually, the dust of Levels 9 through 4 precipitates in Level 3, drifting and sifting into new configurations. These new configurations are formed by Will/Tao/Maat into the most efficient shapes needed for the work of the Supernals.

What can be learned from the Abyss?

That our sense of self is woven and projected from our various levels of density, and possesses no objective existence in itself. That the matter-energy universe and all its reflections on rarer levels are illusion: gratuitous, arbitrary, fractal and beautiful musings of a Divine Intelligence. That the point of Magick, mysticism, initiation, and spiritual seeking is the discovery and sharing of this secret.

One of the statements in Maat Magick is that the experience of the Abyss isn't a single-shot proposition. As you reintegrate your distilled levels with Level 10, care must be taken to prevent old bad habits and viewpoints from reestablishing themselves. The Abyss must be crossed day by day, minute by minute, as a way of life, since Level 10 is a powerful forgettery.

Its sheer density weaves a spell of conviction, as does its consensus-reality generated by the mass of uninitiated fellow humans. In the press of dealing with the thousand details of living, we can forget that all this is illusion, and that we are illusion also. A daily dose of the Abyss maintains mindfulness of truth. To help reassemble your cosmic debris into your Daily Mask accurately, swiftly and aligned in balance, construct a symbol of yourself on Level 6 and wear it as an amulet, consulting it at need.

BINAH / UNDERSTANDING

SINCE WORDS AND CONCEPTS ARE CREATURES OF ILlusion, they fall short of depicting reality beyond their sphere of competence. The Supernals are spoken of as three distinct levels; the distinctions are aspects of one thing, but the trifold division allows us to consider the aspects in more depth.

There are a number of classical metaphors of Level 3: Understanding, the Great Ocean Mother, the City of Pyramids, the Night of Pan, the Vision of Sorrow. I've always wondered about the term "Vision of Sorrow" with its Buddhist connotations. Just because illusion is ephemeral and beauty is fleeting, they need not inspire us to mourn their lack of permanence.

Level 3 is the place where your disintegrated faculties and aspects reassemble as (as Crowley puts it) a pyramid of dust in the City of the Pyramids on the shore of the Great Ocean beneath the Night of Pan. A wind arises from the Abyss and wafts your dust back across the Abyss to settle in that level of density from which your talents best suit you to operate.

While such metaphors evoke certain imagery, they must be understood to be metaphors.

Level 3 concerns the reassemblage of your onion layers in the light of your new understanding of the illusory nature of all things. Although you need to remember the quirks and inclinations of your physical body and how they influence your rarer levels, you are free to reshape your personality, or Daily Mask, on the inner and on the outer.

The "you" I address no longer exists; indeed, it never did. The conventions of language are false above the Abyss, so please bear in mind that we can only hint at the truth in words.

In Level 8, you created and danced various masks, increasing your versatility and range of effective communication. In doing so, you loosened the bonds of identification with your self-concept for serious play, much as children can adopt the personae of cops and robbers, Ninjas, princesses and pop stars. Dancing the mask gave you a range of experience and viewpoints other than those of your "normal self."

In Level 7, you invoked godforms to identify with them. In the process, you expanded your self-concept into the archetypal realm, becoming that which we've worshipped over the ages. If you invoked successfully, you became the god you called, looking upon yourself from a god's-eye view. You experienced being the Other, the not-you.

In Level 6, you invoked and embraced the Holy Guardian Angel. Whether you consider the HGA to be your Higher Self, a Perfect Master, an extraterrestrial "alien," or any spiritually superior being, in invoking it, you aligned your individuality with and merged with, something larger and wiser than yourself.

You also opened to your True Will, an ongoing force larger than the universe, a wonderful Mystery Tide sweeping through every aspect of your being and carrying you onward to the Abyss.

In Level 4, in attaining the double consciousness of N'Aton, your "I" cast loose its moorings from a single skin and skull to become the human race at large. Your sense of self expanded to include all possible expressions of human capacity—from sublime genius to deliberate stupidity, from saintly sacrifice to genocidal cruelty, and all the countless shadings between.

From this comprehension of the human species—past, present and future—as self, as N'Aton, you may have gathered hints of further organization of complexity. As N'Aton, we are members of the Comity of the Stars, an interstellar organization of intelligences that is, in turn, included in an intergalactic organism—and so on.

The point of your experience in the various levels is the dilation of your sense of self to include the plenum, the All. The point of your experience of the Abyss is to discover the Nothing in the heart of the All as you discover the Nothing in the heart of your individual self-identification.

Level 3 is the state of non-density in which your non-physical parts reconstitute themselves in new ways. The first layer to appear around a core of Nothing is will. It's no longer accurate to call it "your True Will," since there is only one will inherent in the plenum of illusion. This will is the basis for existence, the decision of the All to emerge from Nothing and to proliferate forms of variety in abundance.

The second layer is exuded from the first. This second layer is love, the unity of all things in their illusory nature. Love is the singularity that anchors the exfoliation of existence, the focus of the fractal froth of complexity formed by the ongoing extrusion of simplicity.

The third layer to form is the Divine Intelligence that determines the laws of shape, relationship, qualities and behavior of the All and its details. It's this Intelligence that molds the Universal Pattern of Consciousness in everything. It is the factor of existence that increases with complexity and connections, that authors the constants in math, geometry, physics and chemistry, that operates in evolution and decay, that encourages diversity.

Around these layers the levels of density re-form in their progressive order, then the whole of your reconstituted psychic self slides into your physical body and clicks into place. The time that it takes to reassemble varies—more than weeks, less than years.

The traditional title for Level 3 is Understanding. You have a radically different view of life and reality now, but what do you do with it? Level 3 has much in common with Buddhism, in that you see that human suffering and struggle derives from ignorance. Your own denser levels are still subject to pain and loss, but your new understanding of their illusory nature also allows you to experience them without despair and helplessness.

From your initiatory journey through the levels arises a profound compassion for those individuals who haven't seen the nature of reality. The only conscionable course of action is to help the illusory others to come to their own liberation.

Obviously, this isn't done by sitting in a shrine and dispensing your benevolent wisdom to all comers. Rather, you do what you can to help people get into shape and readiness to receive illumination when it touches them. This means feeding the hungry, sheltering the homeless, protecting the vulnerable from violence and doing the necessary to relieve worry and fear for immediate survival. It also means moving our collective self, the still-sleeping N'Aton, to philosophies and practices to reverse pollution, bad management and greed.

In another aspect, the duties of Level 3, which shade into the duties of Level 2, consist of shaking up the complacent, disturbing the satisfied and knocking the props from under the smug.

The most deadly and stubborn barrier to initiation is thinking you already have what you need. The persistence of institutional religions is at once a major cause and a major effect of human spiritual stagnation.

Many people regard religion as a set of family, tribal, or national traditions that serve as social cement and as a means of establishing one's respectability. The more devout see religion as a means of salvation or connection with a higher power, a way of transcending a troublesome life and securing a painless afterlife.

The founders of religions are the followers of charismatic geniuses with psychic powers. The central figures are often raised to divine status by their followers, either through misinterpretation of the figure's own statements, or through the loyalty and grief of the followers after the departure of their leader.

The original followers often gain sacred status in the minds of new generations raised in or converted to the cult in question. The transition from a cult to a religion comes with an increase in numbers and the acquisition of political power. Religions are also characterized by an official priesthood that can range from autonomous group leaders to an elaborate international hierarchy.

Religions that foster private mysticism are small and rare. Most demand faith from their membership: not only faith in the founder and the deity that founder represents or incarnates, but also in the doctrines promulgated by the hierarchy and in its pronouncements. Most priesthoods are supported by their congregations. (Nice work if you can get it.)

If you weren't reared in an established religion, I strongly suggest that you not only study a few, but also attend services of various denominations and speak with the congregational leaders. This is necessary for understanding the present human condition.

Denigrating or denying the validity of a person's religion will only make him or her rise to its defense. An initiate doesn't nail theses to cathedral doors; a pointed question here and there or a censor-bypassing work of art will provide the needed opening for doubt.

Atheists and agnostics often make a faith of science, or more rarely, art. If a person makes a serious pursuit of either, chances are good that s/he will encounter enough mystery to encourage the realization of the unreality of appearances. Unfortunately, many atheists and agnostics grow as comfortable in their unbelief as religious people are in their faith.

The point and importance of initiation is personal experience of reality. Faith is taking someone else's word for it and accepting second-hand information for truth.

Faith appeals to human sloth. Belief is easier than knowledge; it fosters dependence on authority and indefinitely delays spiritual maturity. Belief is safer than initiation; if all your moral choices are prescribed in advance by a cookbook of commandments, you don't have to agonize over decisions.

It's no coincidence that a major Western religion abounds in images of sheep and children. Initiation is difficult, dangerous, and requires getting your hands dirty. You assume profound risks and responsibilities in pursuit of the unknown, with no one to blame but yourself if you fall.

Is it compassionate to open doors to initiation for the confused, the desperate, the ignorant, the comfortable? If you're in Level 3, you know the answer.

CHOKMAH / WISDOM

THE DUTY OF LEVEL 2 IS TO SPEAK YOUR WORD. IN THE smaller sense, your Word is your *Logos*, an entity that is your essence and your child, a distillation of your spiritual experience.

During the Abyss you discovered the illusory nature of your individual identity, so in a sense, "your" Word speaks itself through your composite levels of density. In this sense, your individuality is the instrument of the Divine Intelligence expressing a facet of itself in a unique way.

In the larger sense, your Word *is* the Divine Intelligence, since you are the Divine Intelligence and your Word is your essence. The degree of universality of your Word's manifestation depends directly upon the degree your illusory self can render itself absent in the speaking.

No matter how advanced you are on the path of initiation, no matter how exalted your attainment of levels of rarity, your various bodies, including your physical body, will tend to thicken and obscure your awareness.

The illusory self is a necessary instrument in the realm of illusion. It needs to be much more flexible and obedient to will above the Abyss than it was in its natural state. It functions as your daily mask, but no longer thinks of itself as "the real you."

A wise daily mask nimbly removes itself when information is downloading into and through its individuality. The function of the small self/daily mask/individuality is to translate and transmit the information received in the way best suited to both the information and its audience.

The aim in speaking your Word is the balance of truth and understanding. A truth in one level of density can be (and often is) a falsehood on another level. Your potential audience is a mixed group of people with varied degrees of experience in the exploration of the levels. In what way can you speak your Word to maximize its truth/usefulness and minimize its falsehood/detriment?

Step One: Your daily mask practices constant silence in all its levels. This is an active, listening silence that doesn't strain to hear, but rather waits in patience and attention. What it waits for is not necessarily a literal word composed of letters, although it can be.

The incoming information can be visual, a panoramic view of your experiences, insights and proven intuitions. It can be unlearned knowledge suddenly present in your mind. It can be a montage of omen and metaphor with a bouquet of emotional overtones. It can be music, wordless but precise, singing the beauty of the cosmos.

You'll know it by the way it fits you and fills you simultaneously, evoking a delighted "Of course!" as your response to it.

Step Two: Pay attention to how the information appears in each of your levels. Density obscures; with increasing density, the need for precise metaphors increases. Your transmission of the information should speak to as many levels as possible.

Whatever means you choose to express the information to your audience, seek always to demonstrate as you tell.

Step Three: Speak in the language of your audience, as much as the information permits. Touch the common points of human reality in the telling.

Step Four: Make your Word available in the telling to the widest possible audience; publish, exhibit, play, perform, lecture, and confide. Be subtle, intriguing, seductive, humorous, but never didactic, arch, or strident.

Step Five: Live your Word; "to thine own self be true." Show is better than tell. This step is the essence of Level 1.

In order to avoid the frustration arising from the inadequacy of words or deeds to completely express reality, accept the frailty of your media and your mind from the beginning.

A good approach is to get in the same "channeling state" you were in when you received the information of your Word. This relieves your mind of the burden of trying to process knowledge that's beyond its capacities. A tape recorder and/or paper and pencil should be on hand to catch it while it's hot. Don't edit anything as it comes from you, or permit your "critic" or your "censor" to comment on or come near it. The initial recording of the information of the Word can be used later in its translation into art.

The Word of the Aeon of Maat is IPSOS. It derives from the Latin *ipse* (same) and *os* (mouth or bone). In *Liber Pennae Praenumbra*, the extension of IPSOS, the phrase "By the same mouth. . ." occurs a number of times, connecting apparently conflicting ideas.

The word "mouth" relates to the letter *Pé* in the Hebrew alphabet; *Pé* has the value of 80. *Pé* connects with the tarot trump, "The Tower." In the Thoth Deck, The Tower card features the mouth of Dis.

In the Forgotten Ones, our survival urges and instincts, hunger ranks as the most primitive and basic among them. The mouth is also a talisman and symbol of, as Louis Martinié says, "your place on the food chain."

Maat Magick imbues everything a mouth can do. Consider its range of functions and delights.

It's useful to consider the other reading of IPSOS; that is, "by the same bone." The phrase, "flesh of my flesh, bone of my bone" conveys the essence of unity and kinship.

Our bone, our skeleton, is the center of our fleshly being. Like the hollow center of our spiritual being, "the same bone," the same basic structure, links our common humanity. "The same bone" also refers to our collective unconscious that's waking up to the consciousness of N'Aton.

Meditation and contemplation of IPSOS generally yield interesting information. Used as a mantram, it's swift transportation to the rarer levels. As a Word of Power, IPSOS effects manifestations when used properly. Feel free to use it.

Other effective Words are ABRAHADABRA, LAShTAL, KRIM, OM, YHVH, AGLA, QANESHANTATOR, LUTIS NITRA, etc.

You need to find your own Word, even though using other Words works well in your Magick. Using existing Words is good practice for using your own Word when you know it.

A Magickian's life and work belongs to the cosmos, and in particular to the human race. Speaking your Word and its necessary extensions fulfills your moral, spiritual obligation to the universe. Physical and social obligations continue on, in their own realms. Rendering unto Caesar survives until Caesar is no more.

In the speaking of your Word, you become it—sleek, potent and full of meaning. Once spoken and validated in a human life, a Word reverberates forever in the density levels and in the Akashic echo/record. The Akasha is eternal, and can be accessed by any intelligence sensitive to it. Your contribution to it isn't so much an item in storage as it is a strong thread in a weaving.

What remains once the Word is spoken?

KETHER / CROWN

TRADITION HOLDS THAT IT'S NECESSARY TO DIE IN order to attain Level 1. As with many enigmatic sayings, this is true on some levels, false on others, and both true and false in itself.

After speaking your Word, you realize that you've fulfilled your True Will; having fulfilled it, you can release it. In another way: by the same mouth that speaks its Word are the remnants of the speaker devoured. In yet another way: the vibrations of the spoken Word dissolve the fragile filigree of individuality's ghost. True Will melts into the ongoingness of things from which it had arisen and to which it had ever yearned.

What happens in Level 1?

You live as your very own Self, without a will of your own and dissolved in love. Your levels of density function in harmony, forming a channel for the influence of Level 1 to flow, fill, and spill to and from each level, all the way to Level 10.

Level 1 gives an overview of all other levels situated in overlapping landscapes of individuality and commonality. Its prime blessing is perspective, a perspective of the All as you know it, with its parts and variations revealed in their relationships.

Level 1 shows that everything is as it should be, necessary and perfect in its place. Difficult as it seems to accept, this includes evil and its effects. It also includes your battles and efforts, and those of others, against evil and its agents.

Religions are famous for codifying evil in the form of laws and commandments, most of which are valid. Evil contradicts the Forgotten Ones, the survival urges; a healthy person reacts to the presence of evil with combat readiness. We count as evil deliberate violence against the innocent, enjoyment of another's pain and violating the common good for personal gain.

Institutional religion expands the notion of evil into an engine of control over the faithful by the clergy. Oral tradition is recorded in writing and is later declared to be direct Divine Revelation. Theologians deduce the psychology of God from the sacred writings and their own idiosyncrasies, then issue statements about God's will regarding human behavior.

Humans have a penchant for extending their concepts of evil into realms larger than the human. In Christianity, evil has been abstracted and personified as Satan, a fallen angel. Independent thinking and the questioning of authority are the evils of heresy and apostasy, evils committed against God.

In the New Age/Neopagan/Aquarian schools of thought, pollution and environmental damage are the larger-than-human evils committed against the Earth.

Anti-human evils committed by Nature and chance, such as volcanic eruptions, hurricanes, and earthquakes (known as "Acts of God" in insurance policies), or devastating diseases like AIDS, cholera, or cancer apparently carry no guilt in our minds for the perpetrators.

Sins against God carry the danger of eternal pain in a theologically-determined afterlife. Sins against Earth carry the danger of future pain in a scientifically projected physical life. Sins against humans by humans are self-inflicted wounds on the sleeping N'Aton that weaken and diminish all individuals.

In Level 1, sin and its consequences are seen as existing "below the Abyss," in the densities of duality and illusion. All aspects of life and existence are seen to be illusion. But—just because something is an illusion doesn't mean it's unimportant.

If you attain Level 1 while still in your physical body, you are anchored from Level 10 through all the levels of density. You recognize illusion, but participate in it wholeheartedly to the end of promoting that recognition among other illusory individuals.

You may well ask, "If you've seen that existence is illusion, why care what happens in it and to it? Why do Magick, why publish, why speak, if existence is simultaneously illusory and perfect?"

The short answer is "for the sport," or "for aesthetic enjoyment." The long answer begins with the precept that there is no virtue in suffering.

In Level 10, we see humans causing and experiencing pain that need not be. Pain is useful only as an alert and guide to damage, so that the damage might be ended and healed. When pain, on any level, is extended and protracted, it causes damage also.

An honest look at human history shows that pain and evil arise from a mix of ignorance and stupidity. Ignorance can be remedied by knowledge, but stupidity can only be overcome by internal choice. Stupidity is the rejection of information, a stubborn clinging to ignorance.

In Maat Magick, there's an ongoing working called Operation Nightmare. Many individuals are mired in their pain-making/pain-taking misery by their refusal of initiation, their refusal to wake up to their true nature. There's a thread of fear running through this deliberate psychic sleep, a fear of what the state of being awake might bring.

If we make the sleep of ignorance more frightful than the prospect of awakening, the sleepers will arise. How? By means of induced nightmare, confronting the sleepers with their own hidden monsters.

There are two ways of doing this: the first is by forming a mirrored egg around an individual, so that the evil s/he projects is reflected back from all directions.

The second method is to enter the Nightside of the levels of density and bring out the appropriate monster or monsters to confront the deliberate sleeper. The Nightside is entered through the 11th Level of density which can be thought of as existing both as a level "below" Level 10, and as a level in a dimension projected beyond the plane of the other levels.

Kenneth Grant, in *Nightside of Eden*, and Linda Falorio, in the *Shadow Tarot*, present detailed material about the denizens to be found there.

The main point about Level 1 is the truth that everything is perfect and eternal. You know that your own existence and sense of identity is as spurious as the rest of the great circus of illusions, and there is, ultimately, nothing to change by Magick. And yet, after mystic realization reaches from Level 10 to Level 1, Magick originates in Level 1 and flashes down to Level 10 as lightning strokes of will, creating the densities as it flies.

The essence of Maat Magick is that it self-destructs upon successful completion. It has no possibility in it of becoming a church, an order, or an institution. Once it's done its job, it disappears—as do all valid systems of initiation.

Lady Maat, the *neter* of Truth, wears an enigmatic smile like the Mona Lisa. She's aware of her own irony, in being the most relative and fleeting of abstractions while at the same time being the root of all illusion and reality. She's the only goal worth pursuing; she leads you through wild and terrifying territory, thick with dangers and deceit, until you find her waiting in the center of your heart.

Enjoy.

PART

II

PRESHADOWING
OF THE FEATHER

THE COMING OF A BOOK

THIS WRITING CAME TO ME AFTER THE VISION IT describes. It was written in early 1974; I had been introduced to Magick in 1972 through the writings of Aleister Crowley by a friend who called himself Shadow. There was an occult bookshop in the Mt. Adams section of Cincinnati, a shop named The Dawn of Light.

My avid interest in Magick and Initiation led me to spend some time in the DOL, browsing, reading, buying books, conversing with others of like mind who found the shop both haven and meeting-ground. Here I met the proprietor, Frater Ariel, and my good friend and Magickal colleague, Frater S. M. Ch. H., who invited me to make use of his private library.

From the crew of would-be Magickians who habituated the Dawn of Light arose the proposal for the Cincinnati Chapter of the Crowned and Conquering Child, a group to meet for Working purposes, a fellowship of ritualists to perform group ritual. Frater Ariel's charisma, knowledge, and ownership of the DOL made him the natural leader of the group.

The CCCCC had gathered in the Temple room at Oz Farm for a major time-travel Working. There were about thirty of us present, most of whom had links to our previous group incarnation in the Alsace-Lorraine region in the 1700's. This night we aimed to push our self-awareness even farther, to a time in prehistory where we were preparing for the destruction of an island nation.

I was one of three voyagers. Fra. S.M.C.H. was Master of Ceremonies, Fra. Ariel led the power rhythms of two dozen percussionists, and Shadow was one of the guards. Borne back through time on the tides of the beat, we voyagers called out our descriptions of scenery, people, and events as we saw them.

Toward the end of our journey narrative, while still surrounded by the perceptions of Level 9 in the past, I became aware of a new presence in the Oz Farm Temple in Level 9 in the present. The presence radiated power, but threatened no action.

After the ritual was over and the party began, I asked S. M. C. H what he had thought of the Working. He said that he had perceived the presence of an extra person in the middle of the rite, and he estimated that the person was a Magus in grade. We speculated that we'd created a vacuum when we ventured pastward, and that the mystery Magus had taken advantage of this vacuum to visit us from our future. We agreed to say nothing of this, and to await further developments.

Two weeks after the ritual, I was in the DOL. Fra. Ariel gave me two black feathers, saying, "I don't know why, but I'm supposed to give these to you." I thanked him, and brought the feathers home and placed them on the altar. Two weeks later, I was meditating in both my Level 10 and Level 9 Temples, when I heard a voice say, "Call your weapons."

I moved to the altar on Level 9 and called to me the astral bodies of my wand, sword, cup, and pantacle. Holding my weapons/tools, I gazed into the white flame burning about two inches above the center of the astral altar.

A minute speck of black appeared in the heart of the flame, then rapidly expanded until the whole flame burned black, absorbing light. After a moment's pause, the black flame expanded, engulfing the temple and its furnishings. I hung alone in space, galaxies and stars whirling in the vast ringing silence, and the vision began.

LIBER PENNAE PRAENUMBRA

1. In the Akasha-Echo is this inscribed:

2. By the same mouth, O Mother of the Sun, is the word breathed forth and the nectar received. By the same breath, O Counterweight of the Heart, is the manifest created and destroyed.

3. There is but one gate, though there appear to be nine, Mime-dancer of the Stars. How beautiful thy weft and web, a-shimmering in the fire-dark of space!

4. The two that are nothing salute you, Black Flame that moves Hadit! The less and less One grows, the more and more Pra-Nu may manifest. Do thou now speak to us, the children of the time-to-come; declare thy Will and grant thy Love to us!

5. THEN SPAKE SHE THAT MOVES:

6. I hurl upon ye, children of Heru! All ye who love the Law and keep it, keeping Nought unto yourselves, are ye a-blest. Ye have sought the scattered pieces of Our Lord, ceasing never to assemble all that has been. And in the Realm of the Dead have ye begotten from the Dead the Shining One. Ye then gave birth and nourished Him.

7. Thy Land of Milk shall have the honey also, dropped down as dew by the Divine Gynander. The pleasure and delight lies in the Working, the whole surpassing far the Parts together.

8. The Lord of Parts is placed within His Kingdom, as done by Beast and Bird. The land of Sun is open but to Children. Heed the Eternal Child—his Way is flowing-free, and suited to the Nature of your being.

9. A Voice crieth in the Crystal Echo:

10. What means this showing-forth? Is Time Itself awry? The Hawk has flown but threescore and ten in His allotted course!

11. She smiles, as beauteous as Night:

12. Behold, He spreads His pinions yet in flight, showering and shaking forth the Golden Light upon the hearts of men. And wherein doth He fly, and by what means? The Feather and the Air are His to ride, to bear Him ever in His GO-ing.

13. The pylons of the ages are unshaken, firmly are they Set. The Day of the Hawk has but seen its dawning, and will see its due measure according to the Laws of Time and Space.

14. The Voice then spoke:

15. Then has the Vision failed? Do I behold Thee crookedly, thinking Thee to be Whom Thou art Not?

16. She danced and whirled, scattering starlight in her silent laughter.

17. I am Whom I appear to be, at times, and then again I wear a triple veil. Be not confused! Above all, Truth prevails.

18. I am the Unconfined. Who is there to say me nay, to say, "Thou shalt not pass"? Who indeed may say, "Thy time is yet to come," when Time itself is my chief serving-maid, and Space the Major-domo of my Temple?

19. Indeed, O Voice of the Akasha, I am the means by which you speak. By the same mouth that breathes the Air, do words of doubt pour forth. In silence, then, do know Me. For I am come with purpose at this time, to aid the Lovers of the Hawk to fly.

THE WORD OF FLIGHT

20. Who falters in the flight must thereby fall; the greatness of the gods is in the GO-ing.

21. When first ye fledged, Beloved of Heru, the shell which had protected long had broken. Upon the Wings of Will ye ventured forth, gaining strength and power as ye flew. Ye gained all knowledge of the Feathered Kingdom, whereby ye became as perfect as the Sun. The friends and teachers all became brothers.

22. The regal Swan, the Heron and the Owl, the Raven and the Cockerel did aid ye. The Beauty of the Hawk Himself was granted, the virtues of the Peacock, the Hummingbird and Loon. The Eagle did reveal her inner nature and the Mysteries thereof—behold, ye witnessed how, with her Lion, she became the Swan. And the Ibis of the Abyss did show the Knowledge.

23. Ye flew, O Kings and Hermits! And ye fly even now, within the bending loveliness of NU. But there are those among ye, and below ye, who would snare your wings and drag ye from the sky!

24. Look well within! Judge well your Heart! If ye be pure, it weighs no more than I. It will not bear ye down to the Abyss. For Gold is Light, but Lead is fatal unto flying—plumb your own depths, in Truth and in self-knowledge.

25. If aught would hinder thee, it is thy doing. Behold this teaching now within the Temple.

26. So saying, She-Who-Moves assumed the form of the great Black Flame, growing from the central shaft and billowing out into the Void. The Children of Heru beheld in silence, and listened to Her words form in their hearts.

27. Behold! This lens of Stars now turning in Space before ye—men have named it well Andromeda. Through it I flow unto the holy Moodog, and then to Ra, and thence to ye, O Priests.

28. Ye must not rest content whilst in the Kingdom, but strive and so exceed what is done. In Love of the Lady of the North, and in Will of the Prince of the South, do every thing soever. In the power of the Seven-rayed Star do ye comprehend the Beast. And from HAD of the Heart do delight in thy star-arched darling.

29. Do all this, and then, pass beyond. Abandon aught that might distinguish thee from any other thing, yea, or from no-thing. If the fowler would snare thee, leave thy feather-cloak a-dangle in his hand and soar naked and invisible beyond!

30. But now! As priests within the Temple are ye here, as Kings, and Warriors, Magickians all. The Way is in the Work.

31. The Hidden One of the Abyss now gives the two wherein is wrought the Higher Alchemy: supporting Earth is Chthonos—learn it well, and all bonds shall be loosed for the Will's Working. Surmounting Spirit, there is Ychronos, whose nature is duration and the passing-away thereof.

32. The two are one, and form the Kingdom's essence. Who masters them is Master of the World. They are the utter keys of Transmutation, and keys of the power of other Elements.

33. The Warrior Priests received the keys, and placed them within their robes, to hold them hidden well above their hearts. The Black Flame danced and dwindled, becoming small, a quill pen, plumed and pointed. There being naught upon which to write, one among the Priests came forth, and laid his body's skin upon the altar as living parchment.

34. She-Who-Moves wrote thereupon a Word, but shew it not before them. In patience waited all the Kings and Hermits, assured full well of final Understanding.

35. The Feather grew again, and rounded close its edges, becoming to their eyes the Yonilingam. The image came of Ancient Baphomet, the Horned One, who spoke:

36. Of old ye knew the Key of Two-in-One conjoined. Ye have lived and loved full measure as NU and HAD, as PAN and BABALON. The Mystery of mine own image do ye also know, for such a Truth was for the ancient Orders of the East and West.

37. Bipartite has the Race of Man been in its span. The Father and the Mother made a Child. I am the elder of the Children, true—but now the younger rises to His Day.

38. The nature of true Alchemy is that it changes not alone the substance of the Work, but also changes thence the Alchemist. Ye whose Will it is to Work thereby, behold mine inverse image, and consider well its meaning for thy Task.

THE SHOWING OF THE IMAGE

39. From out the Yonilingam drifted forth a cloud, violet and light-shot. In the misty heart thereof a sound arose, vibrating soft, yet filling everywhere.

40. Jeweled and flashing rainbow-lights from wings, there hovered in the midst an humble BEE. Striped gold and brown, soft-haired and curved in form, it shone its eyes unto the Priests and Kings assembled.

41. Spoke then She-Who-Moves from out the mist surrounding:

42. This is the symbol of the Work-to-come. The Great Gynander in its earthly form. The Magickian shall grow like unto the BEE as the Aeon unfolds, a leader and a sign unto the Race of Man.

43. What then of its nature doth the BEE show forth?

44. Behold, it is not male nor female in the singular. It labors forth by day in constant flight, an ego-less do-er, whose Will and the Hive-Will are but one.

45. It gathers up the flower-nectar, flies to Hive, and there, in pure Comm-Union, doth in this very body Transubstantiate.

46. The Nectar is now Honey. Bee to bee, it is transferred, speaking all Hive Mysteries from and to each mouth. By the same mouth that

first ingathered, is the Honey spent, the secret Alchemy within the Centres turning Silver—Gold.

47. The Hive now lives, immortal. With queen and workers, drones and builder-bees, soldiers, fostermothers—all are one. In constant life-renewal the Hive breathes as One Being, for indeed it is. In the Will of the Hive is the Will of the Bee fulfilled. Each in its appointed place, the Bees work out their Will in ordered harmony.

48. The image fades. Now the poised plume moves in dancing fashion, unfolding from the center shaft long wings, transforming to the shape of the dark Vulture.

49. But know, O Children of the Hawk, a Man is not a Bee. He may profit from the image thereof, to learn of Wisdom in the Working. Behold in Me another image for thy heart's instruction.

50. There rose before their eyes the Tower of Silence, wherein the Lovers of the Fire lay the dead.

51. The Vulture form alighted soft therein, and ate the flesh from corpses to the bone. The wind howled, desolate, in this fearsome place, fluttering the cerements about the ivory bones.

52. Silently, the Winged One stared, gore smeared about her beak. Into the eyes of each Priest there assembled, her baleful gaze did search. In perfect peace did they behold her searching, for each, as Warrior, had made of Death a brother. Deliberately, then, she unfolded out her wings, and took to the wind, and soared up from that place.

THE GIVING OF THE WORD

53. Eternity then reigned. Infinite the veil that hung about them.

54. Somewhere, sometime, the veil parted for a moment, and She-Who-Moves strode forth. More comely than mortal woman ever was, She glowed in radiance of pearl and amethyst. Fine pleated linen was Her gown, girded in gold and silver, and on Her head, a nemyss of starred blue. Her crown was but a single plume, free-standing, and in Her hands the Ankh and Wand of Healing.

55. Unto each Warrior-Priest she moved, embraced and kissed them. Then, seated in the midst, she spoke as comrade equally-ranked:

56. Ye have worked well in all that has been given—upon the Tree of Life are ye founded. In Tetragrammaton have ye proceeded; in all the Beast hath given have ye practiced well. Ye have become Hadit, and Nu, and Ra-Hoor-Khuit. As Heru-Pa-Kraath did ye abide in silence. Ye know Pan as lover and as godform, and BABALON is bride and Self to you.

57. The forces of Shaitan have ye engendered, calling forth the nexus of the ninety-three to work your Will. Separation for the joy of Union have ye known, and Alchemy is Science to your Art.

58. For those who know, and Will, and dare, and keep in silence, it goes now further.

59. In death is life—for now as ever has it been so. The Willed Death is eternal—keep it so. Self of Ego, selfson born of Maya, must be slain on the moment of birth. The unsleeping Eye must vigil keep, O Warriors, for the illusion is self-generate.

60. Constant watchfulness is the first act—the Abyss is crossed in minutes every day.

61. If ye would dance the Mask, then mask the Dance. Exquisite must be the Art in this wise; and balance in the Centre be maintained, or else ye shall give unwonted Life unto thine own creations. Tread carefully this path of Working, Mage. A tool, by Will devised, makes an ill master.

62. Now in the Mass, the Eagle must be fed upon what she has shared in making. By the same mouth that roars upon the mountain, is the word-act of No Difference given.

63. And when Will declares, therein shall join the Bee to add the gold to red and white. The essence of Shaitan is nectar here, the Temple is the Hive. The Lion is the Flower, now betimes, the Eagle invokes the nature of the Bee.

64. Within the triple-chambered shrine is the first nectar pooled. The summons of the wand of Pan awakens the portal-opening bliss. And from the third and inmost-chamber, in joy supreme, the Sothis-gift, quintessential Mead, bounds forth to join Eagle-tears and Lion-blood.

65. Solve et coagula. Comm-Union thereby, whereof the Cosmos itself dissolveth, and re-forms by Will. And know, if aught can be so ordered in the Kingdom, that three or more is zero, as well as older Truths.

66. Then stirred the Warrior-Priests, and of their number, a nameless one stepped forth.

67. We know thee, Lady, unspoken though Thy name has been thus far. But say now—what was written on the manskin? What is the word Thou givest?

68. She smiled and drew from out Her robe a parchment scroll, shaped even as a Star. Unrolling it, she turned it roundabout, so all might see.

IPSOS

69. What is this Word, O Lady—how may it be used?

70. In silent wisdom, King and Warrior-Priest. Let the deed shine forth and let the word be hidden—the deed is lamp enough to veil the face.

71. It is the word of the twenty-third path, whose number is fifty and six. It is the unspoken Abode, wherein the Dance of the Mask is taught by Me. Tehuti watches without the Ape; I am the Vulture also.

72. It is the Chalice of Air and Wand of Water, the Sword of Earth and the Pantacle of Fire. It is the hourglass and tail-biting serpent. It is the Ganges becoming Ocean, the Way of the Eternal Child.

73. It names the Source of Mine Own Being—and yours. It is the origin of this sending, that channels through Andromeda and Set. What race of gods do speak to Man, O Willed Ones? The word of them is both the Name and Fact.

74. It is for thee mantram and incantation. To speak it is to bring about certain change. Be circumspect in its usages—for if its truth be known abroad, it would perchance drive the slaves to madness and despair.

75. Only a true Priest-King may know it fully, and stay in balance through his GOing flight. This is all I speak for now. The Book of the Preshadowing of the Feather is complete. Do what thou wilt shall be the whole of the Law. Love is the Law, love under will.

* * * * * * *

Immediately after the vision ended, I began to write in my Magickal Record as the vision replayed, with the Voice helping me with words. The vision replayed a third time, somewhat later, as I painted it in the form of its major symbols.

I gave the typescript to Fra. Ariel for his approval. He advised me to put it away in a drawer since "the world isn't ready for it." Two weeks after that, the Voice told me to send a copy to Kenneth Grant. I was horrified at the thought; he's an internationally-known writer, and I was an ignorant beginner.

Still, I mailed a copy and waited.

In his reply, Mr. Grant asked me how I'd received *Liber P.P.*, and I wrote back with all the details. We've had a long and interesting correspondence friendship, and for a while I was a member of the Typhonian O.T.O. He included much information on Maat Magick in his *Nightside of Eden* and *Outside the Circles of Time*. I understand that he is writing on *Liber Pennae Praenumbra* itself in his forthcoming book, *Beyond the Mauve Zone*.

Meanwhile, Fr. S. M. C. H has included much Maat material in his "Cincinnati Journal of Ceremonial Magick" and in the Black Moon Archives.

It's through the courtesy of such friends that Maat Magick has grown and developed. The sweetest rewards have been the correspondence with those who found Maat Magick useful in their various paths of initiation, and the original work they've contributed to Maat Magick.

NOTES AND COMMENTS

To save us both unwarranted tedium, I'll only comment on those paragraphs or lines that seem to need it. The numbers refer to the numbered sections in *Liber P.P.* Please forgive me if I've incorrectly estimated your level of comprehension.

1. The Akasha is the totality of information in our universe, timeless and complete. We can tap into it on all the levels if we know how to recognize what we see and know where to look. Sometimes Akashic information arrives in our consciousness uninvited and unannounced; a habit of gentle skepticism helps maintain equilibrium during any resulting chaos.

2. "Mother of the Sun" is Maat's title in Level 3. Traditionally, the Sun travels the ocean of Air from sunrise to sunset in the Barque of Ra. Maat's primary element is Air; her symbol is the feather, her Tarot Trump is Adjustment/Judgment, whose sign is Libra, an Air sign. In Egyptian tradition, Maat is the daughter of Ra, even as she is the Daughter in the IHVH formula.

In the IHVH formula, "the Daughter is placed on the throne of the Mother where she enkindles the Eld of the All-Father." The key to this mystery is to consider Mother and Daughter as representatives of their respective generations.

I've often wondered what happened to the Mother after the Daughter took over her throne and her mate, the All-Father. Recently, I've discovered that the displaced Mother is running through the woods, walking invisibly in city streets, having a high old time as the Grandmother.

Perhaps it is the dethroned Mother who is the key to transcending the IHVH formula. The Father stays with the formula to have his Eld enkindled (the old goat!): the Son has procured the Daughter through redemption for the Father. Tradition doesn't specify if the Son weds the Daughter—we can assume it happens when the Father dies and the Son becomes head of the household and the Kingdom.

The Daughter can look forward to her own eventual liberation as Grandmother, but the Son seems limited to become the Father, then hang on 'til grim death. The IHVH formula needs to be revised for the benefit of the grandfathers—and everyone else.

3. The apparent nine gates are the eyes, ears, nostrils, mouth, genitals, and anus. The true single gate is the mouth, leading to the innermost physical system, the digestive system.

A meditation point. When you really think about our physical form, you see we're essentially elaborate donuts, or tori. Through the Magick of complexity and tight folding, the hole of our donut shape is more extensive and elaborate than our skeleto-muscular systems. Our insides are roughly four times longer than our outsides.

From another view, the "Nine Gates" are the senses, and the "One Gate" is our central experiential processor, where data acquire meaning and are woven into their right place in the design of existence. I count the nine senses as: sight, hearing, smell, taste, touch, proprioception, gravitational direction detection, proximity of large object detection, and awareness of others' attention.

4. The two that are nothing is the formula of 2=0, the essence of Sex Magick and of Samadhi. Hadit is the irreducible point of view at the center of the universe.

"One" is the initiate. Pra-Nu is *prana*, *prakriti* and Nuit. The gist is: the more you absent yourself in your work, the more likely are universal meanings to cloak themselves in your words and your art and so manifest themselves.

5. She-That-Moves, and, in other places, She-Who-Moves, is the title of Maat in Level 1, or Kether. The "Tree of Maat" is as follows:

She Who Moves

Mother of the Sun   Ongoing Balance

(Egg of Heru-Pa-Kraat)

Air, the Unconfined   Mask Dancer

Black Flame

Quill Plume   Bee Gynander

Maut the Vulture

Black Pearl in the Crystal Lotus

6. Heru is Horus. The Law is that of Thelema (Greek for "Will"), which reads "Do what thou wilt shall be the whole of the Law; love is the law, love under will." Nought is Nuit—Infinite Space and the Infinite Stars thereof: I.S.I.S.

The children of Heru are addressed as Isis, who collected the pieces of Osiris (corresponding to the Nomes, or districts, in Egypt) after he had been dismembered by their brother Set. Isis conceived Horus with the dead Osiris and raised him in concealment among the reeds in the marshlands of the Nile.

7. The Land of Milk and Honey, the Promised Land, was denied to Moshe, who was also protected by the concealing reeds of the Nile, as a child. The "dropping down as dew" refers to the Biblical manna that fed the Israelites in the wilderness.

8. The Lord of Parts is Osiris, placed in his Kingdom of the Underworld, the afterlife, by the Bird, his hawk-headed son Horus, and the Beast, To Mega Therion, whose *Liber AL vel Legis*, the Book of the Law, marked the end of the Aeon of Osiris and the beginning of the Aeon of Horus.

The Dying God governs the dead. Horus, the Crowned and Conquering Child leads the living.

The Eternal Child is Lao Tzu, and the Way is the Tao Teh King.

10. The Voice says that the Aeon of Horus is only seventy years old, and Aeons are assumed to last 2000 years.

12. She replies that the Aeons of Horus and Maat are running concurrently as a Double Current of Magick. Her natural element of Air and her symbol of the Feather are linked with the hawk aspect of Horus.

13. The Pylons of the Ages are firmly Set, since Set is the Egyptian analog of Saturn, Lord of Time.

14-15. A reference to Crowley's *The Vision and the Voice.*

17. The triple veil refers to trinitary aspects of godforms, such as Maiden, Mother, Crone, and Brahma, Vishnu, Shiva. Truth is Maat.

18. In the Tree of Maat, Air, the Unconfined is her title in Level 5, Geburah.

19. If exercising your freedom of speech creates confusion, be silent and see the truth.

20. This is self-evident to the experienced.

22. The birds are given in their order of densities.

The swan (glyph of AUM) is the light of the Atman; this light is the first layer surrounding Nothing.

The heron, standing on the verge of water and land, is force on the verge of form, Level 2's Logos.

The owl is a bird of night, even as Level 3 is under the Night of Pan.

The raven is a familiar of Odin, who shares in the Jovian nature of Level 4.

The cockerel is a traditional symbol of Martial fierceness in Level 5, as witness the illegal and popular "blood sport" of cock-fighting.

Horus is the hawk in Level 6 as Lord of True Will.

The peacock is associated with various Love Goddesses in Level 7.

Level 8's flash and brilliance of complexity and swiftness is represented by the darting hummingbird.

The loon's cry at evening evokes the moon and the lunar energies of Level 9.

The Eagle is the Alchemical symbol for the female, lunar essence. The Lion is the male, solar symbol. Their union transmutes them into a single entity, the Swan, the AUM, the dissolution of Shivadarshana into Nothing; 2=0.

The Ibis of the Abyss is Thoth/Tehuti, divine Scribe and teacher, presiding over Da'ath, the non-Sphere, the non-level. Da'ath is both knowledge and confusion, which indicates that knowledge by itself can lead astray without understanding and wisdom to balance it in a trinity.

23. NU, or Nuit, is the night sky and *neter* of the universe. She is depicted as resting on her feet and hands, her body arched over the

Earth. She's a solid deep blue, with stars everywhere in her and on her.

Kings and Hermits are the aspects of the Magickian mentioned in *Liber AL*.

The would-be snarers are anyone or anything that seeks to divert, dissuade, or block you from doing your True Will. One of the greatest snares is to mistake desire-driven attraction for True Will.

24. Lead and gold are both heavy, but lead is poisonous. The Latin word for lead is *plumbum*.

25. The emphasis is on "doing," rather than on "*thy* doing." There comes a time when you have to listen to your HGA and allow events to happen through you without editorial comment or trying to *do* it.

27. The moondog is Sirius. Maat describes part of the route taken by the Magickal Current in the course of its flow. Ra is our sun.

28. Lady of the North: Nuit. Prince of the South: Hadit or Set. The seven-rayed star is the star of BABALON; the Beast here is Pan. Hadit and Nuit are referred to a second time.

29. Three pieces of good advice. Pass beyond: we never arrive, since there's no there there. Our business is to go. Distinguish: work for the Vision of No Difference. This is a state in which all things appear equally illusory; no basis for preference can be formed.

Soar naked and invisible: appearances are only that. Where hindrance to True Will appears, install your point of view on the level above it, and resolve matters from the rarer and more comprehensive level.

31. Chthonos is spacetime, matterenergy. Ychronos is the chart of changes through the time dimension. Both are fractal froth complexities.

35–37. The Yonilingam is a stylized statue of the male and female genitals conjoined. It represents the union of male and female principles as the creative force of the universe.

36. BABALON is an entity channeled by Aleister Crowley. She is a new godform combining the courage of Joan of arc, the ferocity of Boudicca,

the sexuality of Venus and the rowdiness of a Bacchante. She shares many of the characteristics of Ishtar, and some of the Shakti/Shekina.

Baphomet, or Octinomos, was the alleged "god of the Templars." In the famous image by Eliphas Levi, Baphomet is a goat-headed human figure, seated with drapery in its lap. It has long horns, and a lighted torch rising from the center of its head. Its feet and legs are goatish, hooved and hairy. It has female breasts and an erect phallus. One arm is pointing upward, the other downward; one bears the word "*solve*," the other, "*coagula*."

Baphomet is the image of the hermaphrodite, the androgyne, the manwoman. Gender has never been as distinct as the mainstream moralists assume, and it's growing less distinct as we go.

42. The worker bee is a neutered female. The hive is a reproductive unit, however, with queens and drones produced at need. The gynander exhibits no sexual characteristics, while the androgyne exhibits all. The gynander's sexuality is concealed and private to itself.

Humanity is not about to abandon sex, but we are in the process of changing it radically. The likeness to the BEE lies in the realm of the developing double consciousness and its effect on global socioeconomics, not in the area of individual sovereignty. "Every man and every woman is a Star."

49. A Man is not a Bee, even as the map is not the territory.

50. This refers to the followers of Zoroaster, such as the Parsees, who place their dead in open towers for the vultures. Fire and earth are deemed too sacred for corpse disposal.

54. A nemyss is the Egyptian headcloth that has two lappets hanging below the shoulders on each side of the face.

The Ankh, or *crux ansata*, is a cross with a loop for the top arm. It represents a sandal strap (the business of the gods is GOing) and symbolizes eternal life.

The Wand of Healing is the Caduceus.

56. What was given: *Liber AL vel Legis.*

Ra-Hoor-Khuit is Horus in his Warrior hawk-form; Heru-Pa-Kraath is Horus as a human infant or child, seated on the lotus and his finger (or thumb) to his lips in the Sign of Silence. The combined form of these two aspects are Heru-Ra-Ha.

57. Shaitan is the Peacock Angel, god of the Yezidis. He is an analog for Set, or Saturn, the traditional Dark Gods. The ninety-three is the Magickal Current of the Aeon of Horus.

59. The Ego is the illusion of identity giving itself undue importance in the scheme of things. Slaying it consists of reminding it or re-demonstrating to it the actuality of its status.

60. Crossing the Abyss, or transcending duality, is the essence of Ego-slaying. It needs to be done as a regular practice because the density of the levels lends credibility to illusion, and we fall back into dualistic thinking and behavior.

61. It's vital to be mindful of the illusions of personality as well as the illusions of Ego. Don't believe your own publicity.

62-65. These are technical instructions for the Mass of Maat, which is described in detail in Level 7 in the Practice Section.

68 and 69. IPSOS is the Word of the Aeon of Maat. It has four pronunciations and nine spellings. (This information is probably of more interest to the Gematrist than to others.) The four pronunciations are: IPSOS, IPSOSh, IPShOS, IPShOSh. Among other things, these four pronunciations do interesting things in pranayama meditation: IPSOS—inhale, IPSOSh—hold, IPShOS—exhale, IPShOSh—hold. Again, for the Gematrist:

I	-	10	-	10	-	10	-	10	-	10	-	10	-	10	-	10	-	10
P	-	80	-	80	-	80	-	80	-	80	-	80	-	80	-	80	-	80
S	-	60	-	60	-	300	-	60	-	60	-	300	-	60	-	60	-	300
O	-	6	-	6	-	6	-	70	-	70	-	70	-	X	-	X	-	X
S	-	60	-	300	-	300	-	60	-	300	-	300	-	60	-	300	-	300
		216		456		696		280		520		760		210		450		690

The significant Thelemic numbers I've used investigating these numerations are: 11, 31, 56, 93, 111, 131, 156, 333, 418, 666, and

718. The number 123 = EHEIHE IHVH ALHIM, implying Kether, Chokmah and Binah.

[216] – 93 = 123. Also, [456] – 333 = 123.

123 + 111 = 234 + 111 = 345 + 111 =

[456] + 111 = 567 + 111 = 678 + 111 = 789.

[456] + 333 = 789. Also, [696] + 93 = 789.

789 / 3 = 263 = Gematria

678 / 6 = 113 = the same, as in "the same mouth."

567 / 21 = 27. 21 = Existence, 27 = Purity

[456] / 8 = 57 = consuming (re. mouth), wealth, subversion.

345 / 5 = 63. Also 567 / 9 = 63. 63 = fed (re. mouth).

234 / 13 = 18. 13 = love, unity.

18 = chai (life) my beloved.

[456] – 93 = 363 + 333 = [696]. [216] + [450] = 666.

[280] – 156 = 124 = 93 + 31.

[216] – 131 = 85 = Pe = Mouth (as Pe spelled in full.)

[456] – [216] = 240 + [456] =

[696] – [216] = 480 + [280] = [760].

480 / 2 = 240. 480 + 240 = 720.

720 = 9 x 80. 80 = Pe = Mouth.

At this point we'll have mercy on those who have no acqaintance with or interest in the play of numbers.

70. This refers to the Hermit card in the Thoth Deck, recalling Diogenes' search for an honest man. A Word of Power is not to be squandered on the street, where it wouldn't be understood and

where its power would be dissipated. Show is stronger than tell; let the Word manifest itself through you and your art as fact.

71. There are twenty-two paths on the Tree of Life, traditionally. Fifty-six is the number of NU. The Ape of Thoth is an ape sacred to the god; it's also the imitation of teaching, science, knowledge or Magick. The Vulture is Maut, dark image of immaculate conception, whose mate is the southwest wind.

72. The attributes of the elemental weapons are traded around. The hourglass is time and the tail-biting serpent (Orouboros) is eternity.

73. The source of Maat's being, and ours, is the same mouth, our own mouth, mouth of womb and tomb, mouth of river and cave. The Word creates the mouth by which it is spoken, dilating a doorway in the nothingness, then stepping through it. Meaning, information, and significance are inherent in the structure of the cosmos in all its levels. There is only one thing, and it's very busy. As space and time expand, it gets busier spinning itself into more complexities.

The complexities outpace the expansion 2 to 1 in exponential quantum increments.

This requires intricate folding and coiling (like our cerebrum and intestines), curving into fractal froth, generating complexities and connections among them. The one thing is being everywhere simultaneously, creating space as it jumps beyond its previous points in all directions from its initial point.

The wind of its passage stirs the complexities, sets them rotating. The inevitable collisions of points, lines, and sections generate points of mass which drop below lightspeed and take up the trade of quarks. The plunge of mass into subluminal life generates energy which follows the path of the plunge, a subluminal energy.

We are composed of this one thing; its laws apply to us, in translation, from the superluminal to the subluminal. "That which is above is like that which is below; that which is below is like that which is above." We are essentially hardwired to understand ourselves and the Cosmos, sub- and super-luminary.

Our lack of understanding arises from our prolonged transition from our pre-hom ancestors to the mature and united consciousness of N'Aton. Mind is clouded and impeded by emotions, urges, hormones, and wrong ideas. N'Aton uses the superluminary realm to travel back to us, to give us the concepts and ritual tools we need to speed up the process of our becoming N'Aton.

The Magickal Current originates in the essence of things. As a species, we've been broadcasting our signature to the cosmos since the invention of speech. Since the advent of radio and television, our signal has gained much more power.

Our signature signal returns to us through the galactic lens of Andromeda, augmented and aimed by the Sirius system, and stepped down by our sun. The returning signal is changed by its journey, shaped by the cosmos, augmented by stellar energy and enriched by the information gained from other intelligences.

74. The masses of people faithful to mainstream religions will not welcome the implications of IPSOS for a number of reasons.

There was no fall from grace, no Original Sin, no lost preternatural gifts. "If ignorance were bliss, 'tis folly to be wise." The garden of Eden was our prehuman animal consciousness, too primitive for moral distinctions, too simple for guilt, innocent of the capacity for sin.

We emerged in the animal kingdom as the most neurologically complex species on the planet; we have not fulfilled the responsibilities of this fact. Our development has been uneven. Our science and technology have outdistanced our wisdom, and we pay for this imbalance with the doing of evil and suffering for and from it.

In a sense, we have lost the grace of acting with Tao through the overwhelmingly intimate influence of urges misunderstood and misapplied. No individuality, divine or otherwise, can redeem us individually or collectively. No dying and resurrected divine incarnation can restore us to the grace of seeing God.

Only we can transform ourselves through initiation and hard work. When we learn to cooperate with the nature of things, when we learn to see and understand the nature of things, when we expand our sense of self to include the cosmos, then and only then, will we attain the innocence of living in wisdom. Our grace is that of seeing God in the Universal Pattern of Consciousness and its Divine Intelligence in which we participate.

Maat Magick suggests the term "sacred humanism" for seeing the perfectibility of mankind and working toward that perfection. Individually and as a species, we are not a finished product, nor a fully conscious one.

We invent gods to explain to ourselves the mysteries of life; we invent heaven as a compensation for earthly misfortunes and pain. We invent hell as a similar compensation, one often tinged with vengeance and moral self-righteousness. We invent Satan as an excuse for violating our own ethics, as a tempter responsible for our own leanings to sin.

IPSOS implies the need for a spiritual maturity wherein we become our own heroes, saints, and gods, shouldering the responsibility of our own salvation without benefit of clergy, church, or priesthood.

75. Each Magickian is to function as a Priest, not as intermediary, but as friend, mentor and advisor. Each Magickian is to function as a King; not as one commanding, but as caretaker of one's sphere of influence and those living within it.

GENERAL COMMENT

Liber Pennae Praenumbra is the central document of Maat Magick. The vision provided the content and my individuality provided the form.

In the process of writing it, I criticized the use of the second person familiar with its "thee's and thou's," but kept the archaic aspects as they first manifested. We use this old way of familiar speech in prayer as a gesture of intimacy with God. It's fallen into disuse in common speech, but it still has its place in the High Tongue of poetry. My thinking is that visionary material should remain as it first "comes through."

Liber P.P. is a manual of transformative technology that uses wetware as hardware, the astral net as modem and screen, and initiatory experience as programming. Even the minute amount of electrical energy produced by the human brain is enough to link you with the Akashic Echo, or Record, and with the Magickal Current.

Fra. S. M. C. H. published *Liber P.P.* twice in the Cincinnati Journal of Ceremonial Magick; printed in Issue #1 in 1976, and in holographic copy in Issue # 5 in 1983. After receiving *Liber P.P.*, I experienced a string of ordeals that propelled me into a series of initiations. Other things were written that appeared in the Journal. My life since then has been centered on Magick and changing the human race (like trying to herd cats).

The course of initiation never ends.

PART

III

PRACTICE

BANISHMENTS, FEATHER AND FLAME RITE, CONSECRATION

THERE ARE TWO BANISHING RITUALS IN MAAT MAGICK; the first has an abridged version. Banishment defines your working space and keeps you from being a psychic nuisance to your neighbors. It also gives you a sphere of psychic peace and quiet, and prevents interference from Level 9 and up.

THE EIGHTFOLD BANISHMENT (IN FULL)

Begin facing South, making an "X" vertically before you with the sword or wand; do the same at each directional point.

South: (X) In the name Shaitan

Southeast: (X) In the name Heru-Pa-Kraat

East: (X) In the name Ra-Hoor-Khuit

Northeast: (X) In the name Hadit

North: (X) In the name Nuit

Northwest: (X) In the name Maat

West: (X) In the name BABALON

Southwest: (X) In the name Aiwass

South: (X) (Forcefully) Begone, all elementals out of place.

East: (X) Begone, all malignant entities.

North: (X) Begone, all who work contrary to the Magickal Current.

West: (X) Begone, all ye who would interfere.

Facing South, whirl the sword/wand overhead thrice, chanting:

"Shaitan-Aiwass! Shaitan-Aiwass! Shaitan-Aiwass!"

Hold your weapon at the heart chakra, pointing outward horizontally. Turn 360 degrees deosil, crying "Anathema!"

Again, beginning at the South, make the sign of Earth/"Mark of the Beast" at each station. (Trace the "X" as above, then trace an "O" around it: ⊗)

South: (XO) In the name Shaitan

Southeast: (XO) In the name Heru-Pa-Kraat

East: (XO) In the name Ra-Hoor-Khuit

Northeast: (XO) In the name Hadit

North: (XO) In the name Nuit

Northwest: (XO) In the name Maat

West: (XO) In the name BABALON

Southwest: (XO) In the name Aiwass

Touch sword/wand to earth.

To close the banishment at the end of your working, repeat the name and gestures in reverse order (widdershins) at their proper stations.

THE EIGHTFOLD BANISHMENT
(ABRIDGED)

Because the gestures of the abridged Eightfold Banishment require the use of both hands, instead of using your physical sword or wand, use the sword mudra (first two fingers extended, ring and small finger folded to the palm under the thumb), or the wand mudra (thumb thrust between first and second fingers of your fist) where required.

South: Shaitan. (Trace a large vertical "S" before you, arm extended, hand in mudra.)

Southeast: Heru-Pa-Kraat. (Put right forefinger to lips.)

East: Ra-Hoor-Khuit. (Step forward, arms horizontal before you, palms facing forward.)

Northeast: Hadit. (Touch center of forehead with right index finger.)

North: Nuit. (With right hand in mudra and arm extended, trace an arc overhead from left to right.)

Northwest: Maat. (Hold open right hand upright, place extended left hand above it horizontally, forming a "T.")

West: BABALON. (Extend cupped hands together, palms upward.)

Southwest: Aiwass. (Hold both hands above head, index and small fingers extended.)

Touch the extended fingers to earth.

To close, repeat the name and gestures at the proper stations in reverse order.

THE SIXFOLD BANISHMENT

Below: BES! UNIVERSAL ANCESTOR! LINK US WITH THE DEPTHS OF SPACE. SMALLEST OF THE GODS, BORDERLINE OF ENERGY AND MATTER, ANCHOR US IN THE UNCERTAINTY OF BEING. (Squat so that your thighs are horizontal; extend your arms horizontally to each side, bend your elbows so that your forearms are vertical, your hands in fists.)

South: OSIRIS! FATHER OF US ALL! LINK US WITH THE FORCE OF FIRE. PROTECTOR OF YOUR CHILDREN, SIRE OF THE WILL TO LIVE, CHARGE OUR WILL TO CHANGE. (Cross your arms on your chest, hold an imaged crook and flail.)

West: ISIS! MOTHER OF US ALL! LINK US WITH THE WAYS OF WATER. FIERCE AS THE TIGRESS, SUBTLE AS THE FLOW OF OCEAN, FLOOD OUR HEARTS WITH LOVE. (Bend to the right, the back of your right hand on your forehead. Your left arm is extended behind you, elbow bent, hand toward the earth.)

East: HORUS! ELDER BROTHER OF US ALL! LINK US WITH THE ARTS OF AIR. LIBERATOR OF YOUR SIBLINGS, HAWK-HEADED WARRIOR LORD, FREE OUR MINDS THROUGH WINDS OF CHANGE. (Step forward, arms horizontal before you, palms facing forward.)

North: MAAT! ELDER SISTER OF US ALL! LINK US WITH THE ENERGY OF EARTH. DANCER OF THE MASK OF BALANCE, LADY OF THE SCALES OF JUSTICE, UNITE US IN SHARED WORK. (Hold open right hand upright, place extended left hand above it horizontally, forming a "T.")

Above: HARPOCRAT! UNIVERSAL DESCENDANT! LINK US WITH THE AEONS OF TIME! FOREVER INNO-

CENT, LORD OF SILENCE, EXPAND US IN THE
ETERNAL NOW. (Put right forefinger to lips.)

To close:

Above: HARPOCRAT! COLLAPSE THE LONG AEONS TO
THE INSTANT OF NOW. (Hold time as an energy-ball
between your hands.)

North: MAAT! COMPRESS OUR GREAT PLANET TO THE
ESSENCE OF EARTH. (Hold earth as above.)

East: HORUS! CONTAIN THE WILD WINDS BY YOUR
ART OF THE AIR. (Hold air as above.)

West: ISIS! GATHER THE WATERS IN THE HOLLOW OF
YOUR HANDS. (Hold water as above.)

South: OSIRIS! SUMMON ALL FLAME TO THE FORCE OF
YOUR FIRE. (Hold fire as above.)

Below: BES! DRAW CLOSE THE BOUNDARIES OF INFI-
NITE SPACE TO BE A SMALL SPHERE IN THE HERE
OF THIS PLACE. (Hold space as above.)

Push the energies into a single sphere, then compress it to about a
quarter-inch diameter, then swallow it.

You can envision the volume of this banishment as either a
sphere or an octahedron.

Experienced ritualists will notice that the Sixfold Banishment
uses the form of the quarter-calls, thus doing double duty.

SIXFOLD BANISHMENT

FEATHER AND FLAME RITE

This ritual is the best means of contacting the Maat Current.

Sit comfortably in temple, holding a feather between your mouth and a candle flame. Begin repeating the four pronunciations of IPSOS aloud. (IPSOS, IPSOSh, IPShOS, IPShOSh), in such a fashion that the feather vibrates but the flame remains undisturbed. Let your voice work automatically, while you say the words mentally. Eventually your voice will sink to a whisper and disappear.

When this happens, close your eyes and continue repeating the four pronunciations mentally until they, too, disappear. Stray thoughts will arise during this process; take note of them and let them go, neither fighting them nor following them. When the mantra disappears, you've contacted Maat.

You may or may not experience confirming phenomena at the moment, but you will have a certainty that you've touched truth.

For daily meditation, sit in temple with the feather and flame on the altar, but keep your eyes closed and repeat the mantra mentally. When it disappears, begin it again, over and over, until your predetermined time has elapsed. Don't be concerned about your body rocking, twitching or having muscular tics; they're signs of releasing stress and will eventually diminish and disappear.

By using the mantram of IPSOS in twice-daily meditations as a regular practice, you give yourself repeated exposure to Maat as eternal truth. This exposure changes you on all levels of density, makes you healthier, reduces your stress levels, quiets your mind, clears your inner vision, and prepares you to bypass the ordeals of your initiations by opening your consciousness for more accurate perception.

CONSECRATION-DEDICATION RITE: 93/MAAT

The celebrant should bathe and rinse the body with traditional hyssop water as a pre-ceremonial ablution/preparation. If hyssop isn't available, select another herb for infusion, an herb that is indicated for purification and/or refreshment.

The temple is appointed and arranged as follows: The altar is bare; the circle, which is the boundary of the universe, is scribed astrally. About its circumference are arranged the following:

To the South, the wand and candleflame.
To the West, the chalice and a vessel of water.
To the North, the pantacle and a small mound of earth.
To the East, the sword and the feather.

Central is a vessel of oil (pure olive oil or one's personal scent): small quantities, in appropriate containers, of salt, rice and milk; one's "badge of office"—robe, crown or ring; a vessel of wine.

Enter naked.

Approach the circle from the South, arms extended before you, palms facing forward. Walk the circle deosil (clockwise), and at the East assume the gesture of Harpocrat (index finger or thumb to lips). Banish according to the method of your choice. Face the center of the circle and proclaim:

DO WHAT THOU WILT SHALL BE THE WHOLE OF THE LAW.

BY THE SAME MOUTH THAT DECLARES THE LAW, SHALL THE WILL BE SPOKEN AND THE WORK BE VOWED.

THELEMA! AGAPE! ABRAHADABRA! IPSOS!

Extend the arms upward, palms to the sky.

TO NUIT!

BY HADIT!

IN THE NAME OF RA-HOOR-KHUIT!

Proceed to the South; stand before the wand and candleflame, facing outward. Take up the wand in the right hand, pass it through the flame; hold it aloft, saying:

THIS WAND IS THE WEAPON OF MY WILL. IT IS THE PHALLUS OF MY SPIRIT, THE SCEPTER OF MY KINGDOM.

Turn to the center of the circle, pour a few drops of oil upon the wand, and return to the South, facing outward. Rub the oil into the wand; as you do so, chant the name SHAITAN-AIWASS—loudly at first, then diminishing to a whisper. Breathe the whispered name into the wand as you anoint it. Then:

IN THE NAME SHAITAN-AIWASS, I WILL WORK FOR THE MANIFESTATION OF THE LAW OF TRUE WILL. I WILL WORK FOR THE ESTABLISHMENT OF TRUTH, BALANCE, AND JUSTICE IN THE KINGDOM. I WILL WORK FOR THE EVOLUTION OF THE UNIVERSE.

Keep silence for a space, then, with wand in hand, proceed to the West. Place the wand before the chalice. Take up the chalice, rinse it with the water, then hold it aloft, saying:

THIS CHALICE IS THE WEAPON OF MY LOVE. IT IS THE KTEIS OF MY SPIRIT, THE GRAAL OF MY KINGDOM.

Proceed with the anointing as with the wand, this time using the name BABALON-MAAT. Then:

IN THE NAME BABALON-MAAT, I LOVE THEE, NUIT, ALL THAT IS AND IS NOT! I LOVE THEE, LORD PAN, GOD OF LIVING BEAUTY! I LOVE THEE, MAN, SLEEPER IN THE NIGHT OF PAIN AND MADNESS.

Keep silence for a space, then with wand and chalice, proceed to the North. Place the weapons before the pantacle. Take up the pantacle, rest it upon the earth, then hold it aloft, saying:

THIS PANTACLE IS THE WEAPON OF MY BODIES. IT IS THE WORD OF MY SPIRIT, THE SEAL OF MY KINGDOM.

Proceed with the anointing as above, using the name NUIT-HADIT. Then:

IN THE NAME NUIT-HADIT, I AM KING AND MAGE, I AM PRIEST, HERMIT, WARRIOR, AND FOOL. I AM THE DANCER OF THE MASK: THE MASK CONCEALS NOTHING.

Keep silent for a space, then with the three weapons, proceed to the East. Place them before the sword. Take up the sword, touch it to the feather, hold it aloft, saying:

THIS SWORD IS THE WEAPON OF MY MIND. IT IS THE SENTINEL OF MY SPIRIT, THE WARRIOR OF MY KING-DOM.

Proceed with the anointing as above, using the name HERU-RA-HA. Then:

IN THE NAME HERU-RA-HA, I KNOW THAT WE DREAM AS WE DANCE. I KNOW THE LAW THAT GOVERNS THE PLAY OF THE DREAM. I KNOW THAT I AM AS MUCH ILLUSION AS THE REST OF THE DREAM.

Leaving the weapons assembled in the East, return to the center. Anoint the chakras with the oil, saying:

(Base of spine): I DEDICATE AND CONSECRATE MY BODY OF FLESH TO THE GREAT WORK. I WILL KEEP IT IN STRENGTH AND HEALTH TO THIS END.

(Genitals): I DEDICATE AND CONSECRATE MY ASTRAL BODY AND SEXUAL POWER TO THE GREAT WORK. I WILL MAKE LOVE ONLY UNDER WILL, AND ALWAYS TO NUIT.

(Navel): I DEDICATE AND CONSECRATE MY ETHERIC BODY AND MY CHI TO THE GREAT WORK. I WILL FIGHT AS WARRIOR AND BROTHER, AND WILL STRIKE LOW AND HARD.

(Heart): I DEDICATE AND CONSECRATE MY COMPLETE IDENTITY, INNER AND OUTER, TO THE GREAT WORK.

ALL THAT I AM, YEA, TO THE LAST DROP OF BLOOD I POUR INTO THE CHALICE OF OUR LADY BABALON.

(Throat): I DEDICATE AND CONSECRATE MY SPEECH AND SILENCE TO THE GREAT WORK. I WILL SPEAK ONLY TRUTH, AND KEEP SILENCE FOREVER WITHIN.

(Third Eye): I DEDICATE AND CONSECRATE MY VISION TO THE GREAT WORK. I WILL BEHOLD ALL THINGS WITH CLARITY, MAKING NO DIFFERENCE BETWEEN ANY ONE THING AND ANY OTHER THING SOEVER.

(Back of skull): I DEDICATE AND CONSECRATE MY TRUE SELF TO THE GREAT WORK. I WILL ACCEPT MY NON-EXISTENCE, AND AGAIN BECOME TAO.

(Top of skull): Silence.

Put on the ring/crown/robe. Take up the vessels of salt, rice, and milk. Beginning at the South, cast a few grains/drops beyond the circle at each compass point, saying:

TO THEE, SHAITAN-AIWASS, ARE THE KINGDOMS OF THE KINGDOM.

(West): TO THEE, BABALON-MAAT, ARE THE KINGDOMS OF THE KINGDOM.

(North): TO THEE, NUIT-HADIT, ARE THE KINGDOMS OF THE KINGDOM.

(East): TO THEE, HERU-RA-HA, ARE THE KINGDOMS OF THE KINGDOM.

Return to the center with the vessels. Take the wine to the East. Pour wine into the chalice. Take up the wand, and proceed with VIIIth degree, making sure that the elixir flows onto the wand.

Transfer the elixir to the wine; using the wand, stir to commingle. Dip the sword-point into the chalice, so the fluid runs down the blade. Spill a few drops on the pantacle. Turn to the center of the circle, holding the chalice in the left hand, the wand in the right, and declare:

I WILL PURSUE THE GREAT WORK TO ITS COMPLETION. I WILL CONTINUE FROM LIFE TO LIFE, FROM WORLD TO WORLD, YEA, UNTIL THE END OF TIME, UNTIL THE EVOLUTION OF THE UNIVERSE IS COMPLETE. THIS IS MY WORK, MY WORD, MY WILL, MY LOVE. ABRAHADABRA. IPSOS.

Drink from the chalice, to the final drop. Place the weapons on the altar.

SO MOTE IT BE. LOVE IS THE LAW, LOVE UNDER WILL.

Close your banishment after spending some time in contemplation.

NOTES

If you're a beginner in ritual, you'll need to procure your Magickal tools/weapons. The wand is traditionally of hazel, ash, or oak, but can come from any strong tree that radiates power. I once made a wand from a lightning-struck locust tree, and another from a cliff-side cedar. The right tree will draw you to it. Spend some time in silent meditation with the tree, then ask its permission to take your wand from it. When you're aware of its consent, cut a straight length of smaller limb. The wand should reach from your elbow to the end of your fingertips, and should be the diameter of your thumb.

Take the time to thoroughly peel off the bark and scrape the wood smooth. When the wood is dry enough, anoint it with oil and breathe your energies into the wand as you rub the oil well into it.

Your chalice can be metal, glass or ceramic. You could even carve it from wood if you have the skill. If there's no way you can make it yourself, you can buy your chalice. The silver and glassware section of a department store, or a church goods store are likely to provide what you're looking for. Polish your chalice with a soft cloth, taking your time about it, and breathe your energies into it as you polish.

Traditionally, Magickians use swords and Witches use athames (knives). In practice, the length of your blade matters little, as long as it's sharp. Its affinity is with the air and sharp analysis. Again, it's best if you can make it yourself, but if not, your sword can be purchased. If you buy a previously-owned sword, cleanse it by plunging it into the earth, rinsing it with water, drying it in fire and smoke it with incense. Polish it with a soft cloth and anoint it with oil, breathing your energies into it as you do so.

Your pantacle is a disk of wood, wax, metal, clay or ceramic, with the symbols of the universe and yourself as you see it marked, pressed, or carved on it in some way. You should make the pantacle yourself, or at least scribe your own symbols on it. The symbolic universe you choose to represent should have your personal symbol or symbols included. For rites concerning another person or thing, make a talisman with symbols specifically related to the person or thing.

After you've mastered Level 6 and attained Knowledge and Conversation of the Holy Guardian Angel, make a new pantacle. Your symbol choices will have changed to reflect your integrated self. It may happen that other weapons will signal to you that they should be replaced or reconsecrated, but this is rare. Frequent use of your Magickal Weapons in ritual will keep them charged and potent.

Regarding some terms in the Consecration-Dedication rite: Phallus = penis, Kteis = vagina, Graal = Grail, legendary cup said to contain the blood of Jesus, brought to England by Joseph of Arimathea, and sought by the Knights of the Round Table. Other legends say it's in France or elsewhere in Europe.

Aiwass (sometimes Aiwaz) is the praeterhuman intelligence who dictated *Liber AL vel Legis, The Book of the Law*, to Aleister Crowley; he/it is also Crowley's Holy Guardian Angel. Shaitan, the Peacock Angel, is the dark god of the South, is Set, is Hadit, is Saturn. We tend to shrink from his energies because he is Stern Necessity, inevitability, and the mystery of death.

Heru-Ra-Ha is the combined form of Ra-Hoor-Khuit and Heru-Pa-Kraat.

VIIIth degree is autoerotic sexuality. Sex Magick is an integral part of Maat Magick since it makes available a tremendous power for the working of will. Sex Magick is the alchemy of which the old images of alembics and athanors were metaphors. Your physical body is the best alchemy lab available. It manufactures chemical compounds that defend it from microbial and viral infections, that regulate its own growth and stages of maturity, that give its brain endorphinal pleasure and that provide the adrenaline strength to deal with danger.

When sexually aroused, male and female bodies secrete complex fluids that are active physically and astrally, charged by the DNA's will to replicate and change itself in combination. These fluids are imbued with the force of the Forgotten One of racial continuity; they also carry the force of intent when generated in Magickal ritual.

It's best to begin your exploration of Sex Magick alone, so that you have mastery over its inner processes and understanding of its dynamics before you attempt to work with another person. There are two major parts of Sex Magick: arousal to sublimation and arousal to orgasm. With sublimation, you take the energy of the arousal and turn it inward and upward through the levels of density to the end of inducing visionary trance. The sexual fluids are retained or reabsorbed at the source; their energy in transferred to the cerebrospinal fluid that bathes the brain and spinal cord and is drawn upward by the rise of Kundalini.

Kundalini is a force inherent in our spinal cord and brain that usually remains partly inactive. It can be fully activated by a number of practices including controlled breathing (pranayama), concentration and visualization, mantra meditation, etc. Kundalini is connected with the chakras, and can be induced to rise in stages by activating each chakra in ascending order. The chakras can be activated by being mindful of them during work of all types in the levels of density. Some people find it helpful to dedicate a crystal to each of the chakras, charge it by keeping it on the altar during Magickal Workings appropriate to its level and chakra, then by placing it on the body's chakra area.

Although Kundalini sometimes arises spontaneously, traditionally exercises to awaken it are assigned to Level 4. The process can take years to complete, even when assisted by VIIIth degree (many aspects of Magick can be worked reciprocally), so be patient with yourself. The second part of Sex Magick is more immediately accessible.

With orgasm, you take the energy of the arousal and turn it outward and downward into Level 10 to the end of manifesting your True Will through the intention of the particular working. In addition to their own potency, the sexual fluids carry the power of the chakras in them, providing a superb substance for anointing and charging Magickal objects like talismans, amulets, and sigils, as well as sacramental elixir for the strength and health of the Magickian.

There are many books about Sex Magick available, but experimentation and experience are the best means of mastering technique. The success of VIIIth degree work depends on your ability to concentrate mentally, emotionally and astrally on your symbol for the Working in progress, be it sigil, godform, or image of the intended result. It's important to enter all information about each rite (and its results and/or fallout) in your Magickal Record.

In the past, Sex Magick was restricted to the "upper grades" of initiation for a number of reasons, not the least of which was Church doctrine condemning any type of nonreproductive sex. This condemnation created a social atmosphere of restriction, guilt, and fear, and encouraged a general ignorance of sexual potential that was called innocence or virtue. We still encounter echoes of this restriction in laws against public nudity, in the use of sexually attractive models and actors to sell products that have nothing to do with sex, in the pornography industry and in homophobia.

In my opinion, Sex Magick can be used safely by newcomers to Magick if certain principles are held and observed.

—Approach sex with reverence, awe, and love, since it is holy and powerful. We would not exist without the force of this process, without the strength of this survival instinct that can induce us to rear and care for its natural results—children—through a cubhood that lasts twenty years, more or less.

—Remember that every orgasm produces a "child" on one level of density or another. Casual, "secular" orgasms obtained without a dedication to a willed purpose produce children that haunt the lower astral planes, hungrily seeking life force wherever they can find it.

—Orgasms induced to quiet desire or to participate, in love, with another person's desire should be dedicated to Nuit, or to the general intention "to the Great Work" (*in finis* the same thing). This gives the energy sufficient purpose and earthing to prevent it from creating astral monsters; beyond that, each such generation and dedication of energy builds up your Body of Light.

We come to Magick as sexual beings. To delay using our sexual powers in our Magick until we've attained a particular Magickomystical milestone makes no sense to me. Not every ritual employs Sex Magick, but those that do will assist your understanding and progress along the path of initiation.

MOONCUP RITE, THE FORGOTTEN ONES INVOCATION

SOME OF MY FRIENDS HAVE COMPLAINED ABOUT THE difficulty they have in getting started in the exploration and mastery of Level 9 as the astral planes. When I was beginning the practice of Magick, I was inspired to do a lunar rite that had the effect of opening wide my own astral gate. Since I lived in a conventional Midwest neighborhood with no outdoor privacy in the back yard, I drove to a forested city park that was officially closed after 10 P.M.

I parked my car several yards from the entrance drive, and walked in, carrying my ritual gear under my cape. The full moon's light was strong enough for me to find the ring of seven pines that I had noticed in a previous, daytime, visit. On the way out of the park after the ritual, I encountered an officer of the law who asked if my car were mine. I said that it was and commented on the beauty of the night. He said not a word about my being in the park after hours, and we went our separate ways peacefully.

THE MOONCUP RITE

Materials: wand, chalice, sword, pantacle, stick incense, feather, bottle of pure spring water, containers for small amounts of milk, white rice and salt.

This ritual should be performed in the light of the full moon, preferably outdoors; adjust what's given here to your own situation.

Banish. Light the incense and walk with it deosil (clockwise) around the circle. Place the incense (safely) on the ground. Face the moon and lift your arms in a curved position, like the horns of a crescent moon. Pitch your voice quietly but with resonance and say:

LADY NUIT, HAIL! BRIGHT WITHIN YOUR BODY BURNS THE PURE COLD FIRE OF THE MOON, CHANGING IN ITS CONSTANCY, YOUR HEART, YOUR EYE, YOUR WOMB.

LADY ISIS, HAIL! HORNED CRESCENT ON YOUR CROWN, YOU RULE THE TIDES OF TIME AND NIGHT. OPEN TO ME NOW YOUR REALM THROUGH PORTALS OF YOUR SILVER LIGHT.

TRIPLE GODDESS, HAIL! MAIDEN IN YOUR WAXING NIGHTS, AT FULL THE MOTHER ON YOUR THRONE, GATEWAYS TO OUR DREAMS YOU ARE, INTO THE DARK OF WANING CRONE.

Take your blade and cut into the earth two crescents facing inward and a circle between them. Stick the feather upright in the earth above the full-moon symbol. Pour the water into the chalice, offer it to the moon above, then spill a few drops on each symbol, saying:

On left crescent: KHONSU! MOON-LORD, HAIL!

On full moon: SIN! MOON-LORD, HAIL!

On right crescent: CHANDRA! MOON-LORD, HAIL!

Replace the chalice, then take a handful of the white rice and sprinkle it on the left crescent, saying:

DIANA, MAIDEN HUNTRESS IN THE WOOD, I OFFER GRAIN OF PUREST WHITE TO SUSTAIN YOU ON YOUR COURSE.

Pour a few drops of milk on the full moon symbol, saying:

HATHOR, MOTHER COW AND LADY OF THE SYCAMORE, I OFFER MILK OF PUREST WHITE IN HONOR OF YOUR NURTURING.

Sprinkle a pinch of salt on the right crescent, saying:

HECATE, QUEEN OF WITCHES AND GUARDIAN OF THE GRAVE, I OFFER SALT OF PUREST WHITE, A TREASURE OF THE UNDERWORLD.

Pass the incense over each symbol, fanning smoke on each with the feather. Take up the chalice, turn your back to the moon. Catch her reflection in the water, open your soul, and when the moon's image has infused the water with her essence, close your eyes and drink it all.

Pause for as long as it takes to experience the moonlight flooding through your veins. Put the chalice on the ground, turn to face the moon, gazing at her intently; raise your arms in the crescent-gesture and say:

LUTIS NITRA.*

When it seems appropriate, scatter the rice, milk and salt on the ground near the symbols. Clapping your hands softly in rhythm, dance away the symbols and the offerings.

Close banishment, gather your materials and depart.

---

*See glossary.

MOONCUP

ON THE FORGOTTEN ONES

Civilization, law, governance, and good manners form a fragile veneer over the survival urges in the human unconscious. As a species, we've taken great pains to distinguish ourselves from the rest of the animal kingdom. Darwin's evolutionary theories were condemned by Churchmen, and even today Creationists argue for equal time in the classroom. These antievolutionists must have a difficult time with recent genetic findings that humans share 98% + of their genes with chimpanzees.

A classical definition states that "Man is a rational animal." We are capable of reason, but reason rarely prevails in love and/or war. Most human actions and reactions are directed by our survival urges, with reason providing rationalizations to satisfy the conscience. Intellect and Ego delude themselves into believing they rule human life, governmental decisions, and social interactions.

I call our survival urges the Forgotten Ones (FO) because our intellects tend to forget them or to trivialize them. Our individual and collective Egos are artifacts of intellect; it's Ego's vanity that blinds intellect to the power of the FO.

When we contemplate our own lives, we can recall many situations where the FO directed our decisions and our intellect and/or will castigated us for them later. The only way to rein and ride the horses of instinct is initiation.

The time to approach the Forgotten Ones is after discovering your True Will, after meeting your Angel/Higher Self and integrating your waking consciousness with it, balancing the two factors into a third, more enlightened you.

Rooted and hardwired in our neurosystem, our urges are incredibly powerful and authorative; they are not to be opposed or frustrated, but directed to work in ways determined by will in the light of intellect and intuition. To do this, you have to meet the urges on their own deep territory, and become them so you can understand them from inside.

This meeting and understanding can be instigated by the Invocation of the Forgotten Ones. Proper timing is vital to the success of this ritual; if attempted before integration with the Angel, the FO can take advantage of your interest in them and dominate your life entirely. If you neglect to integrate the FO after integrating with the Angel, their frustrated pressures will distort your work on Level 5 and serve to confuse your knowledge.

The ritual deals with the primary urge of hunger (Muladhara Chakra). Hunger is older and more powerful than sex; even amoebae and paramecia, who reproduce by fission, engulf food and digest it. Since hunger is the basic FO, invoking it will provide you the key for becoming and understanding the others. The ritual context will contain any and all of the FO, be it done fully, with concentration, and by an integrated ritualist.

If we look to the rest of Nature, we see hunger in action among all living things, including photosynthetic plants and parasitical fungi. The various food chains depend on the innate urge of the few and the large to consume the many and the small, with reproduction rates to match. Of course, one large corpse provides for many small insects and bacteria, so the energy exchange cycle continues, the bass note of the symphony of life.

The sex urge (Svadhishthana Chakra) is about as powerful as hunger, since it's necessary, in complex organisms, for the continuation of a species and the maintenance of variation within a species. The human sex urge is particularly strong, since it must persuade us to assume a plus twenty-year commitment to child-rearing.

Human complexity adds subtle factors to the sex urge, making it more complicated and powerful while narrowing its focus. Undifferentiated spontaneous arousal is soon directed toward a particular person, or type of person, to particular situations or scenarios, or to symbolic objects. In Sex Magick, use your imagination to employ your complications in building a charge.

The fight-or-flight, or self-preservation, instinct (Manipura Chakra) provides an emergency flood of energy in times of danger. It responds to situations of danger to others as well as to threat to oneself. I've read of feats of superhuman strength in rescues, where a small woman lifts the end of an automobile from a child who would otherwise be crushed, or a man subdues a charging bull to save a group of picnickers. It can be roused in ritual to add power to certain types of Magickal Workings, and it can be channeled and controlled by practice in the martial arts.

When activated in a crowd, this FO can trigger a mindless panic stampede, or turn law-abiding citizens into a lynch mob. When directed by an accepted authority and honed by intensive training and conditioning, fight-or-flight binds armies to a commitment to victory and renders war possible.

Since we, as a species, have killed off most of our visible predators, war has been one of the ways we've discovered to thin out populations and keep our numbers somewhat limited (but not limited enough).

The clanning instinct (Anahata Chakra) binds family, clan and tribe into survival groups and can be expanded beyond these groups to include our species—with considerable difficulty. In order to transcend the primate xenophobia that accompanies the clanning instinct, we must apply intellect, will, and love in equal measure.

In our current world scenario of ethnic bigotry and hate, the clanning instinct combines with fight-or-flight to produce the evil "Us Against Them" mind-set. These two FO also combine to produce heroic rescue efforts. When a person identifies with a particular group, s/he is responding in a rudimentary way to the future double consciousness Maat Magick aims to activate. Unfortunately, partial group loyalty necessarily excludes those who don't fit the group definition, and creates a spiritual division within the individual members of the group.

Initiation requires an inclusive view of clan or family, covering not only humans, but all of existence: the other life-forms of Earth and the planet itself, our solar system, galaxy, universe, and cosmos, and all that inhabit it.

The urge to communicate (Visuddha Chakra) is younger than the first four FO; it arose from the sex urge and the clan instinct, but only came into its full intensity with the capacity for complex thought. Our ancestors had preverbal communication of gesture and sound, much as our contemporary cousins, the apes and monkeys, use today.

Was it coincidence that we developed the vocal apparatus of larynx, mouth shape, and tongue mobility in time to satisfy the communication instinct's need to express abstract thoughts? The FO are powerful and sometimes blind, but in their purity are far from stupid. The invention of speech and the use of symbols (which later developed into writing) were manifested as the will of the FO of communication. This urge is the gateway to the younger, cephallic FO, all of which developed in response to abstract thinking.

The FO of curiosity (Ajna Chakra) drives science and technology, creates myths and theories, and is the gateway to initiation. We see curiosity in other life forms, like bears, cats, and monkeys, but in humans, curiosity joins its power with the power of the preceding FO and the intellect.

Although survival can benefit (or suffer) from the results of curiosity-driven science and technology, this is a side effect of the urge to investigate, to know, to discover the workings of our bodies and minds and of the cosmos. In a sense, curiosity is a higher octave of the sex drive in its search for otherness and its desire to unite with the unknown through knowledge.

Curiosity is the first FO of the mind itself, based upon and liberated by the success of its more primitive colleagues. It draws the sense of identity from self-concern to self-reflection, creating and destroying the ego. It apprehends the dimension of time and yearns to know the future. It rewards the support of its more primitive colleagues by finding numberless ways to ensure individual and collective survival, safety and comfort.

Despite its relative youth and cerebral/abstract nature, curiosity is as strong and powerful as any other FO; indeed, at times curiosity can override hunger, sex, and self-preservation.

The FO of the religious impulse (Sahasrara Chakra) is the urge to go beyond the ranges of sense and thought, to find and join a higher intelligence, a transcendant reality that calls to us from beyond the veil of appearances.

One of our problems with religion is that it can't be achieved through the conventional means developed by our ancestors: e.g., by faith, intellectual theologies and a priest-congregation relationship.

True religion, *re-ligatio*, rebinding, is an individual quest through initiation for personal transformation. The urge to unite with the unknown takes us beyond the realm of the other FO, who are concerned with our safety and continuity in existence. Uniting with the unknown seems risky and dangerous to the older FO, but curiosity and communication support it. The religious urge concerns itself, in part, with postmortem survival; in this, it's harmonic of the three oldest FO.

The final FO is the whole that is greater than the sum of the parts which are the other Forgotten Ones (Bindu). Inasmuch as it is a harmonic of the clan instinct, this FO could be called altruism; in the light of its nature as a total and blend of all our basic motives, it could be called compassion.

When rightly ordered (Maat) by will and understanding, the FO work in harmony to power our Magick. When kept in the darkness of ignorance and aversion, the FO can combine and clash in confusion, directing our actions to evil. Hunger + fight-or-flight + clanning = war. Individual FO can be twisted into evil imbalances: hunger can show itself as greed or avarice, sex can develop jealousy, clanning can manifest tyranny and oppression.

In the Abra Melin Operation, the binding of demons is done by command and authority. In the Forgotten Ones rite, our urges are aligned by paying attention to them, getting inside them, and exposing them to True Will.

On the Outer, the FO are controlled by satisfying them in ritual and in harmonious living. Spend some time contemplating their workings in your life.

INVOCATION OF THE FORGOTTEN ONES

The ideal site for the ritual is out of doors, in a wild and isolated spot where your privacy is assured. If you must work in your indoor temple, procure a brazier or footed cauldron and enough bricks to support it. Be sure to ventilate your temple and be sure your wood is dry and appropriately sized for the container. I'll describe the rite as an outdoor working; adapt it for indoors as you will.

Begin a fast from solid food at midnight before the ritual, and abstain from orgasm for a week. The ritual should begin shortly before sundown.

Materials: wand, sword, chalice, pentacle, jug of water, bottle of wine or other liquid sacrament, sleeping bag and pillow, drum or other instrument. Provide substantial food and drink for after the ritual. If you're a vegetarian, bring a raw root, such as carrot, turnip or beet; if not, use a portion—4 to 8 ounces of raw meat (not pork or fish).

Pick a ground-altar site on a level, open area and dig a firepit to the west of it. Gather your wood and kindling, making sure that it's dry; place it in the pit and arrange it for lighting. Unroll your sleeping bag to the east of the ground-altar, head toward the north.

Banish, then scribe a circle in the earth with the tip of your sword, a circle with the altar, firepit, and sleeping bag inside. Drum and chant as the sun sets. Continue until it's full dark, then light the fire.

Purify with water your hands, mouth and genitals. Pour the wine/sacrament in the chalice and drink, leaving half in the chalice. Take other sacraments as you will. Drum and dance until a trance state descends on you, then put aside the drum and kneel before the altar and fire.

Place your hands on the earth and say:

DO WHAT THOU WILT SHALL BE THE WHOLE OF THE LAW.
ABRAHADABRA.
IPSOS.

Pick up your Wand and hold it with both hands.

MAAT, I INVOKE YOU!
CLARIFY MY VISION, BRACE MY HEART,
AND LET ME LEARN THE FORGOTTEN ONES.
BLACK FLAME, I INVOKE YOU!
VULTURE MAUT, I INVOKE YOU!
BY THE SAME MOUTH THAT CALLS THE FEATHER
IS THE ESSENCE OF THE OLD GODS TASTED.

Place the pantacle in the center of the altar, then allow a few drops of blood to fall on it from the meat (or a few drops of vegetable juice). Repeat the process with the wine/sacrament in the chalice. Place the meat (vegetable) on the pantacle, thus identifying it with yourself.

Begin chanting:

IPSOS, IPShOS, IPSOSh, IPShOSh

At this point you have a choice of either VIIIth degree or drawing a few drops of your own blood as the chant deepens your trance. Envison the Black Flame dancing and obliterating the Universe.

Transfer a portion of the elixir or blood to the flesh (or vegetable) offering, and a portion to the chalice. Move to the North, facing South across the altar.

At the length of your armspan, thrust your wand upright into the earth at your right (West) and your sword point-down at your left (East). Lie prone on the earth, with arms outstretched so each wrist touches, and is bound by, the respective weapon. Concentrate your perception into the rock strata below you. Begin chanting the sound of hunger (a whining growl) into the earth.

As you chant, feel the hunger induced by your fasting and remember the meat (vegetable) on the pantacle, and how tasty it is, full of nourishment and juices. Reinforce the triangular lines of power and attraction—from the FO of hunger that you're invoking, to the hunger within your body, to the food on the altar—while maintaining

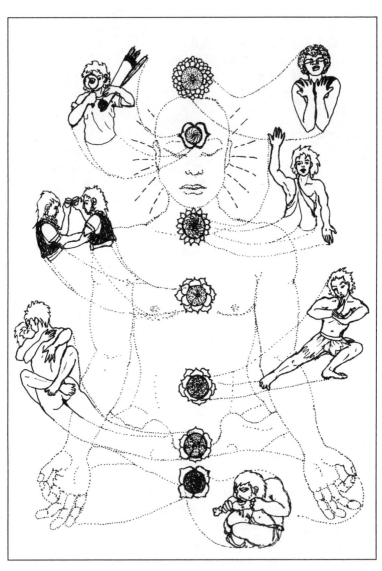

THE FORGOTTEN ONES

a parallel awareness of the binding forces on your wrists from the wand and sword.

Whine/growl as you stir your hunger to a frenzy, restrained by mind (sword) and will (wand). When the intensity of your desire for the food reaches its peak, throw yourself open to the Forgotten Ones.

They will come through the gateway of your hunger, devouring you, forcing your body to its knees. They will lunge you toward the altar, restrained by wand and sword. Project your consciousness into the elixir-food and the elixir-wine, then command your weapons to release your body. The hands will pull the weapons from the earth and violently cross them again on the earth to the South of the altar.

The body crouches above the altar and the food. Your consciousness within the elixir-meat (vegetable) and elixir-wine surrenders to the hunger and other FO within the body—and is consumed. Pause to feel your stomach welcome the sacrifice, then eat enough of the nonsacramental provisions to satisfy the hunger, but no more than that. When you've finished, say:

LOVE IS THE LAW, LOVE UNDER WILL.

Crawl into the sleeping bag and assume a fetal position. The working continues, with no conscious direction, as follows. The Forgotten Ones, inhabiting the body as personified entities by means of your invocation, and thus by your conscious mind and will, have devoured the food and drink that had been charged with the elixir or blood. The elixir, itself, produced by the integrated consciousness and inhabited by this consciousness, is the invoked essence of Maat as the all-consuming Black Flame. You (in the charged food and drink) are eaten by the Forgotten Ones (who inhabit your body through invocation). The Forgotten Ones are eaten by the Black Flame (in the elixir). The Black Flame is eaten by the body. This leaves a vehicle full of nothing, through which the Tao/Magickal Current may flow unimpeded.

As you lie curled in darkness, let the current bring each FO before your attention. Spend the night by the altar. When you awaken, shrink the circle to fit your body and aura, gather your materials, and depart. Enter the rite and its results in your Magickal Record; track all manifestations.

NOTES

There are many other things to do in and with Level 9; imaging and projecting your astral body, temple Workings and scrying in your Magick Mirror, finding your guardian animal and making covenant with its tribe, exploring the Astral Commons, setting up a Hunting Lodge and knowing when it's necessary, group work in astral construction, etc. Some Magickians spend years in Level 9, which is one reason I'm doing no more than mentioning the possibilities here. The idea is to explore, learn, comprehend, achieve competence—then go beyond.

DANCE OF THE MASK

THE FIRST STEP IN DANCING THE MASK BEGINS WITH
meditation-contemplation of the tarot trumps. I use and recommend
the Thoth Deck. Take time to analyze the symbols and details in
each card, and to synthesize all symbolized aspects into a comprehension of the essence of the card, which must include the balanced
opposition of ideas, and of the web of relationship between it and the
rest of the trumps; then begin a series of ritual temple dances. If
there are no strong arguments for a different course, it's well to begin
with the Fool and work through the trumps to the Universe card.

The second step is the Dancing of the Masks in temple, either
in whole-body spontaneous movement or in the concentrated form
of visualization/gesture (mudra). It's best to dance one trump at a
time, and allow the space of a few days or a week between each one.
Place the trump card on your altar and decorate your temple for the
occasion, as thoroughly as possible. Taped music or drumming is
helpful, provided that it's appropriate to the nature of the particular
Mask.

Begin with a banishment, and a period of contemplation of the
trump. Open yourself to its meaning. If you're using your Astral
Temple simultaneously (an especially good idea for this rite), enlarge
and "solidify" the card enough for you to step into it. Begin your
dance by dancing with the main figure(s); in the course of the dance,
become the figure or figures in turn. Make your movement reflect
the nature or idea of the trump/mask; in a way, it's like mime set to

music. Trust your inner awareness to know when the dancing has succeeded in imprinting the mask into your repertoire of aspects.

The third step is the application of the mask in daily life, in relationships with other people and the cosmos at large. Slip into the mask when you're alone, or with strangers in an appropriate situation. It's not a good idea to call attention to yourself by sporting a new personality every week among people who see you regularly. You need honest criticism to hone your performances; the innocent responses of strangers are your best critiques.

Your experience and insight will tell you which mask is best suited to a given situation. Expect a few miscues, and be prepared to learn, to some extent, by trial and error. Your Daily Mask, or reconstructed "natural" personality, should have something of each of the trumps/dance masks in it, ready to flow into any of them instantly.

This is my own interpretation of the tarot-mask-dancing connection; feel free to devise your own.

Linking Levels 10 and 9 is XXI/Street Carnival/The Universe/Tav/(Saturn). Like Mardi Gras and other carnival celebrations, this mask is an attention-getting glitter and confetti expression of dreams and illusions that underlie the density or heaviness of matter. Its central message is that the larger part of existence lies beyond the physical plane.

On the inner, dancing this mask is the earthing of dreams, visions, and emotions. Your Mardi Gras costume and mask present your hidden self to the universe as you step beyond physical density into the rarified realms of images, ideas, connections, principles, spirits, archtypes, godforms, and mystery.

On the outer, your dance reflects the dance of illusion, and lures those who are ready to search out its secrets. The best means of crafting the Mask of Carnival is to make your work and your play the same thing.

Between Levels 8 and 10 is XX/Group Games/The Aeon (Last Judgement)/Shin/Fire and Spirit. This is the mask dance of the Crowned and Conquering Child, whose work is play. This mask is the essence of science and technology. Taking great pains in an organized way to find out the workings of nature in order to satisfy curiosity is science; earthing the knowledge in practical ways is technology. Both aspects are major parts of human activity, and serve communication by igniting curiosity in another through enthusiasm in oneself.

There are old childhood games like Hide and Seek, London Bridge, and Red Rover that generate a gateway between Levels 10 and 8 through the cooperative participation in acting out ideas. On the inner, this dance eases working with other people; on the outer, it invites participation in and enthusiasm for cooperative information-hunting.

XIX/Maypole Dance/The Sun/Resh/Sun is the mask dance connecting Levels 8 and 9. The Maypole is an old pagan dance of Beltane, in which the dancers twine bright ribbons about a pole in celebration of the phallic power of the Springtime god that gladdens the Springtime goddess. This mask deals with the ambivalence about new knowledge; our curiosity drives us to discover the unknown, but new knowledge often obliges unwelcome personal change. The mask of the Maypole Dancer encourages curiosity, change, and the celebration of new beginnings.

In the Thoth Deck, the Sun card shows two children dancing on a hillside; again, the image of the Child reminds us that this work is play.

XVIII/The Coven Circle-Dance/The Moon/Qoph/Pisces joins Levels 10 and 7. The witch-mask speaks to the possibility of knowing divinity directly, without a mediating official priesthood. It also is a mask of glamor-casting and spell-weaving, captivation, and seduction, and requires a sensitive skill in dancing. It also requires ethical use; its power derives from levels far beyond the simple instinctive response to pheromones and lust. It lures the soul itself.

On a practical level, dancing this mask doesn't require you to dress in black, wear pentagrams and patchouli, and look "witchy." On the contrary; this is a chameleon mask that adapts itself to the beholder. On the inner, this mask calls forth the Goddess and her Horned God as the creative dualism that produced the universe. There is a special emphasis on "lunar" qualities in the dancing: receptivity, reflection, attraction, and other yin characteristics.

XVII/The Royal or Military Procession/The Emperor/Tzaddi/Aries bridges Levels 7 and 9. This attribution has changed places with the Star in the Aeon of Horus; the Emperor formerly connected Levels 2 and 6. The essence of this mask is that of authority and leadership. It appeals to our monkey-nature to trust and follow someone who knows more and has better judgment than we do. The only ethical way to dance this mask is through demonstrations of competence; demanding respect without deserving it fools only the naive, and can lead to disaster for all concerned.

When the occasion arises for you to take charge of a situation, dance this mask. In doing so, you're obliged to consider the greatest good, the highest loyalty, the most efficient ways. The mask teaches the beginnings of the Voice of Power, the True Voice, Ma Kheru. It is not loud, but pitched by your confidence in your competence. The mask also teaches the value of tact in cooperative relationships and in inspiring others to motivate themselves.

On the inner, consider why the New Aeon Emperor belongs in the bridging of Level 7 (relationships, creativity, love) with Level 9 (astral planes, survival urges, emotions), rather than linking Levels 2 and 6.

XVI/Shiva's Drum-Dance/The Tower/Pe/Mars links Levels 8 and 7. This mask dance shatters complacency in the notion of "one of true faith" or "one correct view." It blends science and art in revealing both to be valid, and uses both in conveying the idea that "everything you know is wrong." Ninety percent of Magick is trash-removal, and it's often necessary to destroy in order to build better. It's also necessary to be compassionate in destroying long-cherished beliefs.

On the inner, dance this mask in times of mental disarray, of confusing the planes, of taking metaphors literally; it works well in dispelling illusion.

XV/Punch and Judy Show/The Devil/Ayin/Capricorn is the mask dance uniting Levels 8 and 6. This ancient puppet-show, in its humorous depiction of human domestic turmoil, dances a mirrored mask that reflects an old struggle for control between mind and will.

This mask has attributes of Pan, Coyote, and all tricksters; its dance often requires the unexpected and surprising revelation. In dancing this mask, you often play opposing roles for the other person, arguing both sides of a question, and being the Devil's Advocate with others' ideas and pet theories. The humor of this mask, properly applied, can prevent the arousal of anger or opposition to its process.

On the inner, the dance acquaints you with the comedy of Pan inherent in duality, plus an understanding of panic as a disruptive force.

XIV/Greek Drama/Art/Samech/Sagittarius links Levels 9 and 6. This mask is the classical one of Oedipus, Antigone, Creon, Agamemnon, etc. Its dance leads from the daylight of integrated waking consciousness to the darkside of human nature in the realm of the hidden urges. In dancing this mask, it's sometimes convenient to believe in the old gods who were ancestors of the classical Greek gods, in that the old ones are closely linked with the darker recesses of Level 9. Sincere, even if temporary, belief manifesting through this mask can convince the other person to take the Level 9 darkside seriously enough to deal with it appropriately.

On the inner, this mask can provide the key for your own approach to the control and direction of the survival urges. Your faculties of Level 6 stand godlike in relation to your faculties of Level 9; from Level 6 you can see a wider field of existence and grasp the context in which your Level 9 reality functions, much as an aerial or satellite picture reveals more than can be seen from the ground. Use the essence of drama to convince your Level 9 that this wider field of vision assists survival, and the survival urges/Forgotten Ones will be more cooperative and in harmony with will.

XIII/Cobra-Kiss Dance/Death/Nun/Scorpio is the mask bridging Levels 7 and 6. In India, there are the Naga/serpent worshippers who bring food offerings to cobra dens and dance with the snakes, risking death by kissing them on the head.

The mask dance is correspondingly dangerous, spiritually, in that the religious aspects of Level 7 hold the divine to be other than, and superior to, the balanced Self of Level 6. Conversely, an incomplete attainment of Level 6 can misidentify the Ego with godhood, preventing further evolution. In dancing this mask, you become dangerous and fearsome to your beholder(s); it should be used sparingly.

Death frightens and fascinates us because a certainty and an unknown are united: all living things will die eventually, and none of us knows of our postmortem fate. It's the final (perhaps) Magickal Mystery Tour; we may touch the bones of our ancestors, but only a comprehension of death permits us to touch the bones of our descendants. Mystics speak of dying into the light; sleep is called the "Little Death," as is orgasm. This mask exudes a fascination that few can resist. Its dancing assists others to cast off the restrictions of outgrown ways and visions so that the new can manifest. Consult *The Book of Thoth* for details on the scorpion, the serpent, and the eagle, three appropriate approaches for crafting this mask.

XII/Tribal Pole-Diver/Hanged Man/Mem/Water is the mask between Levels 8 and 5. The modern thrill-sport of bungee jumping is similar in form, but different in intention from the sacred practice of leaping or spinning from a tall pole, feet secured by a tough vine or rope. Traditionally, the Hanged Man signified self-sacrifice for the salvation of others, but in the Double Current of Horus and Maat, the mask dance of the pole-diver represents the calculated risk.

This can take a variety of forms, among which are the appearance of vulnerability and the manipulation of guilt. The latter makes use of pre-existing feelings and does not attempt to create guilt where it doesn't already exist. One of the results of initiation is the absence of guilt and the concept of redemption from it, and to this end you must always work. In an unfair situation, however, this dance can be used to obtain redress for another, provided you employ subtlety and a deft touch in execution.

XI/Kathakali Story-Dance/Adjustment/Lamed/Libra is the mask dance that joins Levels 6 and 5. Religious tales from the Mahabarata, the Ramayana and other sources are brought to life through the sacred dances performed to a narrated or sung text. In practical application, this means "show is better than tell," and a combination of both is best, in conveying timeless truths. Good example in action is often more effective than any amount of arguments or sermons.

The Adjustment card (Justice, in other decks) is the one that directly represents Maat. In the Thoth Deck, she's a masked dancer with a double-plumed headdress, wearing the translucent pleated linen garb of ancient Egypt and carrying the sword of mind/air.

Dance is an art that requires balance and motion, which are attributes of Maat. A mask is an aspect of truth that interprets data in a particular, and therefore incomplete, way. To dance a mask is to share an interpretation of information that emphasizes a particular aspect while implying the wider range of truth that contains it.

X/Sufi Dance/Fortune/Kaph/Jupiter is the mask linking Level 7 and Level 4. Its essence is that of change, and generally counsels patience. The tides of fortune or luck turn and change, and nothing lasts forever. The dance revolves about a single point, and the circling movement generates a trance in which the center is revealed.

In practice, this mask dance encourages a circulation between the levels it connects, between insight and imagination, between intuition and art. When you're dancing it for yourself, it helps to dissolve creative blocks.

IX/Shaman's Medicine Dance/Hermit/Yod/Virgo is the mask dance uniting Levels 6 and 4. In the realm of existence, the integrated self reaches a point in its initiation where its realizations outstrip speech and art, and isolate it. This is a necessary incubation, in silence and solitude, on the inner; outer functioning goes on as it must, with no hint of distraction or lack of attention. This mask dance is vital to the initiate.

It is our tie to Earth, in all important ways. Although each path is unique, as initiates, we do not own our own lives. In the past, we could go apart from our tribes, out to the Spirit Places, and find our powers and wisdoms. This was less distracting than in modern times, but the essence remains that what is done benefits the tribe.

The Mask of the Shaman allows you to dwell in the wilderness as you must at times, while living in the riotous changes of daily life. It enables you to be "completely normal" with those around you while keeping silence in your heart. The great paradox of this mask teaches that when the question "Who am I?" is fully answered, there's no one there to hear it.

VIII/Salome's Dance/Lust/Teth/Leo is the mask dance between Levels 4 and 5. Lust means gusto and enjoyment of life as well as strong sexual desire. The combination of strength and expansion in this mask dance provides a powerful charisma and attraction, and makes your words and intentions irresistible. It can overwhelm other people, and should be danced with awareness and delicacy.

This mask is good to dance for addressing groups and other occasions of public persuasion. On an individual basis, the dance arouses fascination in the other person. It's important that you direct the fascination to the information you're imparting and away from yourself, lest you become the other's object of fixation.

Salome's Dance is a mask that's useful in Sex Magick for either gender. I recommend that it be danced in conjunction with the invocation of a goddess- or godform. This practice will deflect fixation away from yourself and change it into devotion for the godform. In all types of Magickal Workings (or in any of the daughter arts), the more the Ego/self-consciousness is absent, the more effective are the results. While the observer always influences the experiment, the influence can be minimized.

VII/Cossack Horsemen/The Chariot/Cheth/Cancer is the mask dance linking Levels 5 and 3. This is the first mask dance that crosses the Abyss, the unbridgeable gap between essence and existence, Noumenon and Phenomena. The Cossack horsemen perform acrobatic feats of dexterity at full gallop, putting themselves at great risk. Their mask dance is just as risky in its own way, since it involves the Oath of the Abyss.

In essence, the oath says: "I vow to interpret every phenomenon as an encounter of God with my soul." A sincere taking of the oath will transfer you to Level 3, ready or not. I recommend dancing all the preceding masks and exploring Levels 10 through 4 before taking the oath, although it will work from any level. Thorough preparation and practice temper the risks of gyrations at full gallop.

On Level 10, this mask dance reveals the divinity of the other person to you, and gives you understanding of the best ways to reveal that divinity to the person him/herself. It's a useful mask to dance with particularly disagreeable and obnoxious persons, as well as with those seeking counsel. It benefits your own course of initiation by assisting your Abyss-crossing through multiple encounters with the reality you seek.

VI/Pas de Deux/The Lovers/Zain/Gemini is the mask dance linking Levels 6 and 3. This mask derives from the duets in classical ballet where the hero and the ingenue express their love to romantic music. This is another dance that crosses the Abyss; it uses the alchemical formula of 2 = 0.

On Level 10, this mask is often danced as Sex Magick, where the mutual ecstasy annihilates the Magickians' egos and charges the resulting elixir with energies congruent with the intention of the working.

This mask can be danced alone with your self balanced and harmonious on Level 6, and the cosmos as your beloved. Your ego/sense of self dissolves into the cosmos, and your individuality no longer restricts you to its illusion. This mask reveals further meanings of love under will.

V/Religious Procession/The Hierophant/Vau/Taurus is the mask dance joining Levels 4 and 2. On the outer, dancing this mask means creating and conducting rituals involving other people, either singly or in a group. A well-crafted ritual can expand the participants' vision and comprehension, impart to them extraordinary energy and desire for transformation and create a gateway of passage through the Abyss.

On the inner, this mask dance can be vital in your own initiations. The principles of ritual obtain for solo as well as for group workings. All elements of the rite serve to turn the attention of mind, will, senses, and emotions to the stated intention. Energy is then generated and released into a symbol of that intention, energy that is focused and held on target by the total attention directed toward the intention. After a ritual, record it in your Magickal Record, then forget it. This particular mask dance creates a tight working relationship between intuition and wisdom.

IV/Water Ballet/The Star/He/Aquarius links Levels 6 and 2. This mask dance is aquatic since it involves swimming in the Magickal Current in the style appropriate to the Magickal formula that you're working. The Magickal Current flows in the river of time, since time is the major dimension in which change occurs. A Magickal formula can be the aspects of the letters in a god-name such as IHVH (Yahveh), an archetype of primitive experience, as in the for-

MASK DANCER

mula of the Father, Mother, Son and Daughter, etc., or any viewpoint or set of viewpoints appropriate to the Magickal task or intent.

This mask dance helps you to assess situations and choose the appropriate masks for dealing with the people in them. It helps the integrated self of Level 6 invoke and use the wisdom of Level 2. On the Inner, the meaning of He, "window," predominates in dancing this mask, since it penetrates the Abyss, allowing the enlightenment of wisdom to touch the heart. In the other direction, the dance crosses the Abyss by means of immersion in the Magickal Current, responding to its every nuance and enhancing its course. The Magickal Current is the Tao, about which nothing true can be spoken.

III/Pavanne/The Empress/Daleth/Venus is the mask dance bridging Levels 3 and 2. The Pavanne is a dignified dance of the courts of Spain and France, a dance derived from the stately walk of the peacock. This dance is the essence of social grace, of relationships enhanced by nobility of heart. The court of the Empress witnesses no quarrels.

The mask dance of the Pavanne concerns life "beyond the Abyss," and shares energy and connection with the mask of the temple-dancers/High Priestess. The Pavanne joins understanding and wisdom on the outer through courtesy and consideration, though not necessarily with formality. It's "do unto others as you would do unto yourself," because your definition of self has expanded beyond limits and includes all others.

II/Temple Dances/High Priestess/Gimel/Moon links Level 6 and Level 1. The temple dancer has a Shaman-like function in that his or her dances are an act of unity with the gods, an act of respect and honor for the gods, and a sharing of information from the gods with fellow devotees. The aim is to encourage the fellow devotees to dance this mask themselves, since every man and every woman can experience divine transcendence directly. There is no need for clergy among Magickians (especially in Maat, save as colleagues may assist each other.)

On the inner, dancing this mask confirms the connection of your balanced self and That which emanates the cosmos and its levels of truth and density. From Level 6, the dance is inward and outward simultaneously, aware of That in everything, aware of everything in

That. When awareness of the essential holiness of everything is habitual, your life becomes your work.

On the outer, the temple dance mask works like a mirrored veil, showing to others their own images and the divinity that animates the images. Gimel is the camel who crosses the desert of the Abyss.

I/Tightrope Walker/The Magus/Beth/Mercury is the mask dance between Levels 3 and 1. The Magickian walks a tightrope every time s/he directs action for an intention. Magick is illusion, since it can only operate in the realm of duality, below the Abyss. Every time you act upon and with physical reality, mental reality, emotional, creative, spiritual realities, you acquire the densities of the levels you use. This is known as incurring Karma, a very tenacious illusion. (No good deed goes unpunished.)

In dancing the mask of the Tightrope Walker, you learn how to act without incurring Karma through the alignment of your True Will with the Tao. This is a dance of transcendant consciousness, wherein you shape illusion to more accurately reflect truth. All densities are holy, and matter is not to be disdained, since all its forms bear the Universal Pattern of Consciousness.

This mask requires the awareness that all situations are best dealt with from the next level of lesser density in relation to the major level of focus of a situation. On the outer, you dance the alignment of events with the Tao, through understanding how illusion works. This mask carries the responsibility of universal spiritual transcendence.

0/The Mime/The Fool/Aleph/Air is the mask dance between Levels 2 and 1. The essence of it is silence, of being your true Self, of the absence of a dancer behind the mask.

The aim of initiation is to disappear.

It takes more effort than childbirth, carries more power than volcanos, tornados, and earthquakes, and is more fearsome than death. When you disappear, your attributes remain, carrying on your normal activities, sharing intimacies, and functioning as usual, or better than usual. An attribute is anything you can truthfully call "yours," and is therefore not "you."

When you disappear, if you've established good self-discipline in your life, the Tao directs the action of your attributes with no mistakes. I don't know of anyone dancing this mask on the outer, save as the absent dancer behind other masks. As you dance the Mime, you achieve transcendence and its freedom.

· · · · · · ·

These descriptions are my own interpretations of the trump cards; each person undertaking the Dance of the Masks should develop his or her own version of them. It's a good idea to record each phase—contemplation, dancing the mask in temple, and employing the masks on the outer—in order to judge for yourself how accurate and effective each is for you.

DIVINATION

The curiosity factor in humans has led to a number of ways invented to find out information on the past, present, and future that can't be found by ordinary ways of observation, conversation, written records, or reasoning. The methods of divining the unknown range from the reading of animal entrails and observing the flight of birds, to the casting of runes, cowrie shells and yarrow stalks or coins for the I Ching, to palmistry, tea leaf reading, and channeling mediums. The tarot deck has a long history in Western Magick, and is my own favorite method.

I found that the traditional method of the Cross and Ladder layout is sufficient for the usual questions on love and finances, but not for deeper matters of the spirit and the soul. Through experimentation, I found two layouts that answered these deeper matters: the Tree of Life and the Star of BABALON. The first gives a "snapshot" of a situation valid for the time of the asking, while the second is more a dynamic reading of processes and their probable outcomes. I find myself using the first method more often than the second.

When someone asks me to read the cards, I tell the person to concentrate on the question or situation, but not to speak the question aloud. I shuffle the deck briefly, then pass it to the querent with the instruction to shuffle it until it feels ready. I then lay each card in sequence in the proper place, face up.

Each card speaks its meaning relative to its place in the layout and to the other cards; I begin a narrative based on what the cards mean, making note of significant factors, such as a predominance of one suit over the others, or the absence of a suit, what trumps and court cards are visible, and where they are, etc. Usually, in the course of the narrative, I hit a "hot streak" where information beyond that visible in the cards breaks through. I speak this information to the querent also; the process feels like a direct tap into the Akasha.

After all is said, I ask the querent if there are any specific questions about the reading, and if the reading made sense. I don't recall any negative responses to that question.

There are a number of books on the tarot available, and most of the many decks available contain instruction booklets. Facility in reading a layout comes with practice and familiarity with the meaning of the cards. Once you're past needing to consult a book during a reading, the Akashic channel will open. It feels odd at first, and you may doubt the accuracy of what you're getting, but again, practice builds confidence.

TREE OF LIFE LAYOUT

Lay out the cards as follows:

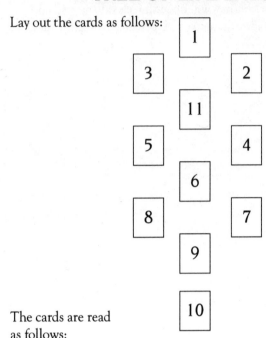

The cards are read
as follows:

1 = The origin or root of the situation;
2 = The nature of the force or forces at work;
3 = The essential form of the situation;
4 = The projected development of the situation;
5 = The power/energy/strength of the querent;
6 = The will or position of the querent;
7 = The querent's relationship with others;
8 = The querent's thinking on the situation;
9 = The querent's feelings/reactions;
10 = The situation's physical manifestations;
11 = What the querent needs to know to deal with the situation.

The majority of querents are interested in finding out about love, employment, family, and health in a situation of uncertainty or crisis. With this layout, you can discern the hidden elements in a situation and give appropriate advice couched in words the querent can best understand.

STAR OF BABALON LAYOUT

Lay out the cards as follows:

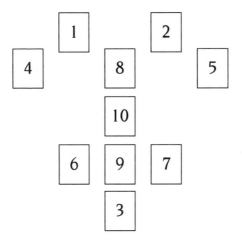

The cards are interpreted as follows:

1 = Nuit: the "universe" of the situation;
2 = Hadit: the querent's point of view;
3 = Ra-Hoor-Khuit: the result/child of 1 & 2;
4 = Pan: the solar/yang forces at work;
5 = BABALON: the lunar/yin forces at work;
6 = Shaitan-Aiwass: the direction of the Magickal Current in relationship to the situation and the querent;
7 = Therion: editorial comment or pointed advice;
8 = Will: the querent's will or its needs for manifesting;
9 = Love: the querent's desire in the situation;
10 = Truth: probable outcome or balance of the situation.

You can add an eleventh card as a significator to indicate the general tone of the querent's situation, or as a symbol of the querent. I usually do, since eleven is the number of Magick, and adds a feeling of completion to the reading.

Once you're familiar with reading the tarot and have proved your accuracy with it to your own satisfaction, there's nothing wrong with charging people a reasonable fee for a layout and interpretation. My own view on the ethics of charging people for a Magickal service is that it's lawful to get paid for your time and expertise. The same holds true for making a talisman or amulet for someone. The only "service" that you should never charge money for is imparting initiatory information, or for spiritual counseling.

Some of my colleagues say that they have other people do readings for them, saying that they can't read accurately for themselves. I've never found it to be a problem; I do find that I hardly ever read the tarot for myself lately, since information presents itself directly, but I trust the deck when I do use it.

THE MASS OF MAAT

AS I'VE MENTIONED BEFORE, SEX MAGICK IS AN EFFEC-
tive means of directing a powerful force to serve the aims of will. Unfortunately, humans have made sex a confusing, troubling process
by linking reproduction with the inheritance of property, power, social status, and kinship claims. Add to this the various religious pro-
scriptions and prescriptions on sex through the ages, the chattel
status of women in many societies even today, and the mighty influence of the sex hormones themselves on thought and action, and you
have not only a source of power, but a touchy and explosive potential
for confusion and devastation.

The description of the Mass of Maat is given in terms of a heterosexual couple, but your creative imagination can adapt it to various circumstances. Both partners should be healthy, clean, and
approximately equal in level of initiation; the aim of the rite should
be fully accepted by both partners, and the rite should be discussed,
contemplated, and prepared for well in advance.

In the Mass of Maat, the woman takes the active role and the
man takes the passive role, even though both are equally involved. If
it's at all possible, perform this rite in your Level 10 temple; if not,
transform your bedroom into a temple with candles, incense and other
items according to taste. Banish thoroughly before and after the rite.
On Level 9, you can choose either partner's Astral Temple in which to
work, or you can image-talk a new one together especially for sexual rituals. This should be established before the actual ritual is begun.

Begin by sitting in Asana or cross-legged face to face, holding hands. Gaze into each other's eyes and synchronize your breathing. Feel two points of energy begin to build between your palms. When the energy grows to two globes engulfing your joined hands, let it flow up your arms, around your shoulders to your necks.

Let the energy divide: one part ascends to your heads, suffuses your brains and shines through your eyes; the other part spreads down your backs and legs, under the soles of your feet, up and around the front of your legs, genitals, abdomens and chests until it rejoins itself at your necks.

Use your hands to activate your partner's chakras, as yours are being activated. Do this by increasing the strength of the energy in your hands, lightly caressing the chakra area. Begin with the back of the head, top of skull, third eye on the forehead, throat, heart, navel, genitals and anus. Adjust your postures as needed.

The man assumes the Corpse Asana, that is, lying on his back, arms at his sides. The woman begins gentle oral sex on him. The man closes his eyes and silently repeats his Word of Power as a mantra, opening his awareness of the chakra on the top of the skull. He feels the inrush of the energy of the Magickal Current enter that chakra, then cascade down through the back of the head, third eye, throat, heart, and navel, then pool as a building charge in the genitals and anus. The two lowest chakras coalesce on Level 9, and link in erotic sensitivity on Level 10, for each partner.

The woman works gently but avidly while opening her lowest chakras and silently repeating her Word of Power as a mantra. The inrush of the Magickal Current's energy is opposite in charge to the man's, a drawing charge, a hungry charge that flows up her chain of chakras, suffusing them all and concentrating in her throat and mouth, with an equal concentration in her lowest chakras.

The next stage depends on the man's stamina and powers of recuperation, and should be discussed before the ritual. If he's able to go a second round within a reasonable time, about a half hour or less, then the woman brings him to orgasm and ingests at least a small portion of the current-charged semen.

If there's any doubt about his recovery abilities, or if there would be too much effort involved in a second round, the woman ceases the oral stimulation after tasting and swallowing the few drops of pre-ejaculate fluid.

After a complete orgasm, the man descends from the no-mind ecstasy into conscious awareness, resumes the silent repetition of his Word of Power and gently stimulates his partner's genitals with his hands until he's ready to rise again. If there's been no complete orgasm, or if he maintains his erection, he continues with his Word of Power and stimulates her orally.

Meanwhile, the woman maintains manual contact with his penis (in either event), and focuses her attention on the energy of the charged fluid/semen she's taken. She absorbs this in her heart chakra, then circulates it from heart to throat, third eye, crown and back of head, then back to her heart to begin again.

This circulation begins slowly, but builds in speed until it reaches its escape velocity, fountains up through her crown chakra, joins with the full force of the Magickal Current of the cosmos, then "rains" back down through her body to join the pooled energy in her two lower chakras. The energy concentrates in her uterus and awaits the next stage.

When the time is right, the woman straddles the man and inserts his penis into her vagina. The movements and rhythms from this point should be left to the wisdom of their bodies. The silent repetition of the Words of Power continues.

While simultaneous orgasms sometimes do happen, they're not strictly necessary for this rite to succeed. It's often helpful for the woman to stimulate herself manually during the conjoined movements to keep in parity with the man's level of excitement and proximity to orgasm. Familiarity with the sexual sequencing of her partner is helpful in this.

At the brink of orgasm, each partner should have the crown chakra wide open to the influx of current. As the cascade of orgasm begins, each partner vibrates his/her Word of Power aloud. If a sigil is being used, it should be called to mind by both partners and dissolved in the rush of pleasure at the speaking of the Words of Power.

During orgasm, the energy of the first seminal elixir flows from the woman's uterus and unites with the fresh semen and her own charged secretions in her vagina.

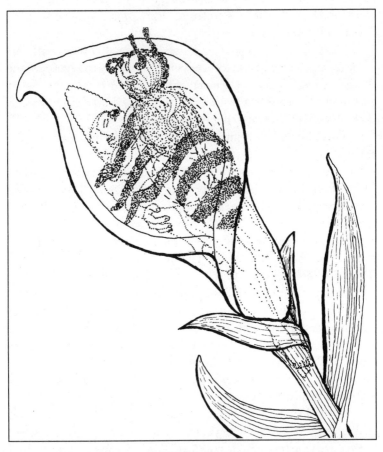

MASS OF MAAT

When consciousness fully returns to both partners, the man extracts a portion of the combined elixir with his tongue and shares it with the woman in a kiss. The rest of the elixir can be used for a variety of Magickal purposes. It can be used to charge Magickal tools and objects, talismans, amulets, and sigils. It can be mixed with ink, paint, clay, or dye for works of art, and can be used to anoint musical instruments, costumes, and computers.

The elixir can be dried to a powder and kept on the altar for long-distance workings by mail, for taking to natural sites, and so on. Fresh elixir is the more potent form.

An extra element is added if this rite is performed during the woman's menstrual period. The resulting elixir, or "Red Gold," can open gateways in Level 9 that are usually inaccessible, can summon strange and monstrous entities, and can speed and solidify results in Level 10. Great care should be taken in using the Red Gold.

One of the major drawbacks of this rite is that it makes "normal" sex seem flat and ordinary. This effect can be partly offset through making all sexual activity Magickal by having an intended use for the energies generated and by using the silent repetition of the Word of Power.

Solo sex offers the opportunity of invoking a god or other entity for Level 9 partnership. One solo technique is performed in bed before sleep. Visualize a sigil you've prepared while you stimulate yourself into heavy arousal, but stop before orgasm. From your Level 9 temple, walk out its door and stand at the edge of the astral commons. The entity or entities will appear from the astral mist to have sex with you.

Devise a test in advance to prove the entity's authenticity. This can be done by demanding a name from the entity and checking it mentally by Gematria, but this is practical only for those who have memorized the proper number values for the alphabet, have memorized significant correspondences from the tables, and are quick and accurate in mental arithmetic.

For those of scant experience in the levels of density, rely on congruencies; if the entity matches the gist of your sigil, if it can articulate the words ABRAHADABRA and IPSOS, and your own Word of Power, proceed with awareness. The Magickal Child of this type of operation is the manifestation of the desire encoded in the sigil.

A less elaborate method is to invoke a god or goddess into your-self, then offer him or her the joy of your own pleasure, giving him or her place in your flesh to experience it. The reciprocal gesture is that the god or goddess sponsors the manifestation of your desire. After you anoint the sigil on paper with the elixir, eat it, burn it, bury it, drown it, or use what method you choose to destroy its existence on Level 10.

If the descriptions in this chapter elicit feelings of revulsion or distaste in you, you aren't ready for Sex Magick and should not at-tempt it. You shouldn't try to sell the idea to your partner if s/he feels the least resistance to it, nor should you allow yourself to be con-vinced against your better judgment, even from the motive of pleas-ing your partner or doing him or her a favor.

INVOCATION OF THE HGA

PREPARATION FOR INVOKING THE HOLY GUARDIAN Angel should include a period of meditation and contemplation of yourself. Your Magickal Record is your best tool in this. Write out the story of your life, with comments on events. List your strengths and weaknesses, virtues and vices, likes and dislikes.

Write what you intend to do with your life, what you consider to be your real calling, why you decided to incarnate this time. Include parental expectations, comments from friends about what they think you're good in, advice from teachers and counselors, and your own opinions about it all. You may have firm answers to all of this and have confidence in your intentions, or you may still be groping for self-knowledge. In either event, begin assembling the materials necessary for the ritual.

Your HGA may have revealed itself to you in the past spontaneously, unbidden, and to your great surprise. In this case, use the rite as a formal reunion to scribe a new pantacle and to prepare for the Forgotten Ones rite.

INVOCATION OF THE
HOLY GUARDIAN ANGEL

Materials: large mirror, placed opposite your altar; blank paper; pen or pencil; blank pantacle of wood, wax, clay or other impressible material, placed near the mirror; wand; sword; cup; gold paint and small brush; 4 gold or yellow candles; frankincense; gold or yellow wine or other drink of a golden color.

Decorate your temples on Levels 10 and 9 in gold or yellow. Place a cushion before the mirror.

Enter your temples, light the candles and incense, then do the Sixfold Banishment. Stand before the altar and say:

DO WHAT THOU WILT SHALL BE THE WHOLE OF THE LAW.

BY THE SAME MOUTH THAT SPEAKS THE LAW IS THE GUARDIAN ANGEL SUMMONED. BY THE SAME MOUTH, O BLACK FLAME DANCING, IS THE TRUE WILL TASTED AND PROCLAIMED.

Take the wand in your right hand and your sword in your left, then carry them to the mirror, crossing them on the floor before it. Return to the altar; bring two of the candles and place them on either side of the mirror. Return and bring the paint and brush. All travel should follow the circumference of the circle. Carry the incense around the circle and return it to the altar. This is all done deosil, as the sun appears to travel.

At the top of the mirror, paint the Utchet, or Eye of Horus: While you paint, chant repeatedly:

ABRAHADABRA.

When you finish the symbol, say:

RA-HOOR-KHUT, HAIL! SUN HAWK, SHINE YOUR LIGHT INTO MY HEART THAT I MIGHT SEE MY DAIMON GUIDE.

At the bottom of the mirror, paint the feather of Maat:

While you paint, chant repeatedly:

IPSOS

When you finish the symbol say:

LADY MAAT, HAIL! FEATHER OF TRUTH, BALANCE ME IN
HARMONY THAT I MIGHT KNOW AND HEAR MY OWN
TRUE SELF.

Align the mirror on Level 10 with your scrying-port on Level 9. Seat
yourself before the mirror and stare into your own eyes, chanting:

SECRET SELF, I CALL YOU.
GUIDING SPIRIT, COME!
GUARDIAN SPIRIT, COME!
NUIT'S LOVE, I CALL YOU.
GUIDING SPIRIT, COME!
GUARDIAN SPIRIT, COME!

Repeat the chant until it fades to silence; continue to repeat it mentally until it fades into the inner silence. As this happens, your eyes
will change their focus, spreading to a wider, softer field. Let this
happen without trying to refocus your eyes.

Your image, and that of your physical temple, will blend and
blur with the mist of the astral commons. Let your heart burn with
longing for the Angel, even as your breathing slows, thoughts cease,
and any strain or striving falls away.

One of two things will happen at this point. An image will appear in the mirror, in which case you will step through the mirror on
Level 9 to embrace it. The alternative is that nothing happens, in
which case you return your consciousness to your physical body,
touch a drop of wine to the rim of the mirror, extinguish the candles
and exit the temple, leaving everything in place until the next occasion to begin the rite again.

Don't be discouraged if this Working takes a number of attempts to complete. Carry the yearning and the chant in your heart
until the next ritual opportunity occurs.

BEING THE ANGEL

When you do see and embrace the image, let it reveal to you what it will, which should include its name. Let the experience flow at its own rate until you return to your physical body.

Return to the altar, pour wine into the cup, then raise the cup in a salute to the mirror, touch a drop to its rim, and drink.

Take the paper and pencil and write the name of the Angel, plus any other words and symbols it gave you. Scribe these on your blank pantacle, return it to the altar, saying:

KNOW THYSELF!

Breathe the name you were given into the pantacle three times, followed by:

IPSOS.
ABRAHADABRA.
BY THE SAME MOUTH THAT KISSED THE SOUL'S OWN SELF, IS ITS NAME GIVEN TO ITS SYMBOL.
LOVE IS THE LAW, LOVE UNDER WILL.

Place the pantacle on the altar, then burn the paper. Close with the Sixfold Banishment, extinguish the candles, and depart the temples.

In the following days, spend as much time as possible in temple meditation with your HGA, consolidating your new consciousness. When you've achieved stability and balance in your new state, begin preparations and plans for the invocation of the Forgotten Ones, as given on pages 131–144 in the Level 9 Practice Section.

COSMIC VISION, VORTEX RITUAL

THE RITUAL PRESENTED HERE DIFFERS SUBSTANTIALLY from the Vortex Ritual first published in Vol. 1, Issue 5 of the Cincinnati Journal of Ceremonial Magick. Since that time, the idea of the Double Current of Horus-Maat expanded to include all of time in the concept of PanAeonic Magick, as presented in the seventh issue of the magazine.

Imagine, if you will, a field of force surrounding the planet Earth, similar in its way to the electromagnetic field detectable by a magnetic compass. This field of force may be considered the astral body of the Earth's physical field, moving along lines of flow parallel to the lines of force in the physical field. This astral field bears the Magickal Current which impinges on it much as the solar wind impinges upon the physical field.

There are whirls and eddies in the Magickal Current at various spots around the globe where the power concentrates. Some of these center on geological formations such as mountains or caves or meteor impact craters; others are to be found at large cities, battlefields or ancient centers of worship.

You can create your own vortex in the Magickal Current centered on your Level 10 temple, your physical body, or both. It will charge your Level 9 temple automatically, since both temples share an inter-level link.

The Magickal Current exists on Levels 4 through 10 and originates above the Abyss in the dimension of the levels. In our familiar
spacetime dimensions, it flows from Earth as well as to it, spinning
from all habitations of self-aware intelligence throughout the universe.

The vortex created by the ritual concentrates power on a local,
terrestial basis, but extends receptivity to various types of information from everywhere. When you discover how to perceive the information borne on the Magickal Current and learn to understand
its content, you'll be able to appreciate the variety life exhibits beyond our carbon and planetary versions.

For practical purposes, however, the local features of the current are what we use to strengthen ourselves and our Magick. Once
you've established your vortex, you can tap its power for any rite or
situation by turning yourself on your own axis, Sufi-dancing style,
while envisioning the forces.

VORTEX RITUAL

Materials: wand; sword; cup; pantacle; iron container, such as a cast-iron "Dutch oven" or cauldron; small magnetic compass; 5 red candles; dragon's blood or cinnamon incense; red wine; talisman of a spiral in black superimposed on an eleven-pointed star in red on rice paper or cigarette rolling paper (cut off any glue). The temples should be furnished in shades of red.

Place the cauldron in the center of the temple floor, your pantacle in the center of the cauldron and the compass on the center of the pantacle. Place the cup, with wine in it, to the North of the cauldron, with your wand in the East and your sword in the West, both touching the cauldron. Stand in the South, facing the cauldron. (All directions are reversed south of the equator.)

Perform the Sixfold Banishment, then cense the circle deosil, or clockwise. Place the incense on the altar, return to the cauldron, and say:

DO WHAT THOU WILT
SHALL BE THE WHOLE OF THE LAW.
ABRAHADABRA.
IPSOS.
QANESHANTATOR.
(Qoph, Nun, Shin, Nun, Teth, Teth, Resh = 718.)

Take up the wand, dip it into the wine, then draw its tip around the rim of the cauldron in continuing circles, deosil, chanting:

GOD HAS A SPIRAL FORCE. GOD IS A SPIRAL FORCE.

Continue chanting and moving the wand around the cauldron's rim as you begin to step widdershins around the cauldron. Stretch your awareness up and out to feel the Current with its diverse streams of energy flowing over, around, and through the Earth, your temple, and you.

Stand in the South; raise your wand from the cauldron and continue its circling overhead. Go to the altar, take up the talisman

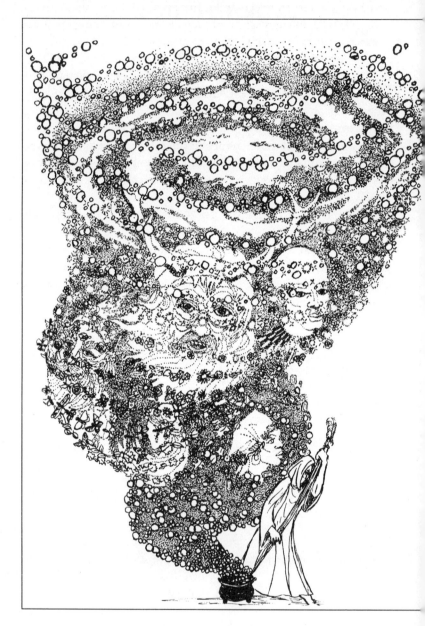

VORTEX

and a candle, return to the cauldron and place the talisman on the compass; take up the sword and move it in concert with the wand overhead, saying three times:

FROM THE DOUBLE HELIX OF THE LITTLE GOD TO THE WHIRLPOOL OF THE GALAXIES, I AM A SPIRAL FORCE.

Put down the wand and sword, and take up the talisman, compass, and pantacle. Hold these in your left hand, point your right hand straight up, arm extended, and turn in place, chanting:

ROTA ATOR ORAT TARO
OTAR TORA AROT RATO

When you feel the Current turning with you, raise the pantacle, compass and talisman above you, gradually slow your own turning. You should be able to perceive the forces of the Current swirling around the temples, as though you were in the calm eye of a hurricane.

Place the pantacle and compass on the altar, then return to the cauldron. Set the talisman on fire, holding it over the cup so that the ashes fall into the wine. Stir the wine with the wand, saying:

BY THE SAME MOUTH THAT DRINKS THE WINE IS THE PROMISE OF RIGHT ACTION GIVEN. BY THE SAME BREATH, O AIR THE UNCONFINED, IS THE POWER COMMANDED AND THE FORCE INHALED.

Drink the wine while it's still spinning from the stirring. Replace the cup in the North, then cross the wand and sword on the rim of the cauldron, and say:

LOVE IS THE LAW, LOVE UNDER WILL.

Close the Banishment, extinguish the candles and depart the temples.

The compass can serve as an amulet of the vortex, although you carry about a natural talisman that works as well or better—the iron in your blood's hemoglobin that circulates in your body.

Experiment with the speed of your rotations to find what's comfortable for you. The fluid and otoliths of your ears' semicircular canals can become disturbed to the point of making you dizzy and imbalanced if you spin too fast. There is a proper trance-inducing rate that you need to find for yourself.

COSMIC VISION MEDITATION

Sit comfortably in your temples, facing East. Close your eyes, slow your breathing, and become aware of your body, the clothing it has on and the chair, cushion, or rug on which you're sitting. Visualize yourself and your seat, and extend your vision to each level of awareness.

Send strands of your awareness into the floor of the room you're in, out to the walls and roof, and down into the foundations of the house or building. Notice the earth and stones surrounding the foundation, plus the pipes, wires, and conduits connecting your structure to others on the street. Take note of the traffic on your street, of your neighbors and of passing pedestrians.

Spread your sense of connection farther still, encompassing your neighborhood, your city, county and state. Touch the clouds overhead, the doings of the winds, the flows of above ground and subterranean watercourses—springs, rills, creeks, rivers, lakes, ocean. Embrace the continent, riding on its tectonic plate, generating an earthquake here, a volcano there, electrical storms in several places at once.

Extend your vision to enclose the entire Earth, tropics and poles, jet streams and horse latitudes, geosphere, hydrosphere, atmosphere, biosphere, noosphere. Ride the turn of the day, the wheel of the orbit, and the call of the moon in her tide-raising link.

Behold the love of the Sun for the planets; its life is our life. Embraced by its gravity, we dance in solar radiance: too little, we starve; too much, we burn. Blessed is our place in the family of the Sun!

Reach out to the other planets, moons and asteroids in our solar system; sunbaked Mercury, Venus boiling beneath her clouds, stark Mars, the scattering of rocks that might have been a fifth planet, then the gas giants with their rings and moons and crushing gravity. Beyond the outlying Oort cloud of comets pours the aged light of stars. Ride the tide of photons to its many origins, blue-shifting in your speed of thought. Embrace our wheeling galaxy as home, then reach beyond to other globes and whirls of light, the cousins of our cluster. See them ringing unlit deeps, a froth and foam of light, afloat on nothing but the song of hydrogen.

Feel the searing blasts of supernovae sacrifice, the atoms of your molecules shivering in sympathy and nostalgia; from starstuff are we made, and at such price! Pretend to mass, then slide down the gravity well of a black hole, where light cannot escape, to cross accretion disk and event horizon to see the other side. Release the pretense, then soar beyond, to realms beyond our sphere of sight.

All this you are.

Blazing with lightstorms among the stars, aloof and lone in the unlit deeps, you are all this. Know thyself.

Remain in your expanded consciousness until you're called back by the needs of your protoplasmic body in Level 10. Slowly contract the field of your awareness until you're sure of your physical control. Gently stretch your body, one part at a time, leave your temples and eat something.

LEVEL 4

PRANAYAMA, ADEPT'S THESIS

THE PRACTICE OF *PRANAYAMA* BENEFITS ANYONE WHO does it, no matter the level of attainment. It's given here in keeping with tradition, and as a basic technique for raising and/or balancing Kundalini. *Pranayama* reduces stress and tension, induces relaxation and promotes serenity. It also leads to the state of no-mind, a necessary condition for the reception of information, power and inspiration.

PRANAYAMA

Sit comfortably with spine erect. Close the right nostril with your right thumb and inhale through your left nostril. Hold your breath for as long as you can without strain, then expel the air through your left nostril, slowly and gently. Repeat on the right. The stoppings of breath are called *kumbhakas*; traditionally, do twenty of these per session, in four sessions per day at sunrise, noon, sunset, and midnight.

In my own practice, I've found it helpful to use IPSOS as a silent mantra as follows:

inhale	—	IPSOS;
hold	—	IPShOS;
exhale	—	IPSOSh;
hold	—	IPShOSh.

In his *Liber HHH*, Crowley gives three imaging meditations for rousing Kundalini that can be used best in connection with the *pranayama* exercises. Do the twenty *kumbhakas* first, then the meditations from *Liber HHH*. Given the suggested schedule of *pranayama*, I found it convenient to begin each session with the appropriate solar salutation from *Liber Resh vel Helios*.

It's helpful to follow a vegetarian diet for the length of the Kundalini Working. It's difficult to predict the length of time needed to fully raise the serpent-power because of individual variation, but figure on a minimum of three months.

The natural activation of the chakras doesn't follow their linear order. The first chakra, the Muladhara, is activated at birth so we may seek nourishment beyond that which had been supplied from our mother's bloodstream.

The third chakra, the Manipura, becomes active in the toddler beginning to explore the world. Its link to assertiveness, territoriality, and aggression is obvious in the "terrible twos (and threes)," when we fight over toys and learn to "just say no" to everything the adults want us to do.

The heart chakra, the Anahata, begins its stirrings in response to parental affection at an early age, and continues its awakening through loving relationships with siblings, pets, and friends.

The genital chakra, the Svadhisthana, awakens at puberty with the onrush of the hormones and physical changes. Normally, the Svadhisthana awakens in the context of the other chakras which help to keep its demands within the boundaries of social acceptability. Many times, the combination of the Anahata and Svadhisthana acts to produce the desire for initiation, to generate a lust for the Divine.

The higher chakras usually need deliberate work to activate them. The Visuddha Chakra of the throat is the seat of expression and the arts, and is partly activated by secular education. The Ajna and Sahasrara require the initiatory attitude to awaken. This attitude arises from the lust for the Divine coupled with intelligence and imagination.

For those who do not cultivate and develop the middle and upper chakras, life is dull, brutish, and usually short. They live to eat, drink, have sex and fight, not necessarily in that order. Awakening and exercising the heart and throat chakras add love and expression to the basic survival urges of the three lower chakras; for those who go no further, life can be noble and satisfying in the intellectual, healing, governmental, and nurturing arts. Some people live lifetimes without acquiring the initiatory attitude; these are the pillars of society, without whom civilization would collapse.

For those who go beyond to activate the Ajna and Sahasrara Chakras, life becomes a conduit of Tao, an ecstasy of dissolution and disappearance into the great mystery of being. The Sahasrara, or crown chakra, is transphysical, and links one's entire self with the energy and intelligence of the universe and beyond. It's a gateway linking our individuality with its source destination.

One method of activating the chakras is to place your consciousness and sense of self in each chakra while you do your pranayams. Visualize your surroundings from your spine at the height of the chakra being awakened. You'll know when it's time to move on to the next one by the cessation of symptoms appropriate to the chakra you've been working on.

These symptoms can appear in you and/or in the people and events around you, giving and receiving. Since it's best to begin with the Muladhara and work up, even though the lower chakras have been partly aroused by ordinary living, you might experience an increased appetite, or invitations to dine increase in frequency, or people give you food, or you change your food preferences. When you witness a settling into normalcy from these unusual events, it's time to move your point of view to the Svadhisthana for *pranayama.*

After odd manifestations of desire and lust, when you move to the Manipura, be ready for symptoms of strange possessiveness, defense and belligerence. At the Anahata, you'll find new levels of affection within yourself and coming to you from other people. Don't allow the symptoms to distract you from your basic task of inducing Kundalini to rise; all these manifestations will pass.

The lower and middle chakras are linked to the spine; the third eye and crown chakras are of the brain. The Bindu, or point, lies toward the back of the brain. This is the focal point of consciousness, and is created, in a way, by the action of all the chakras. It functions as the operator's chair or conductor's podium—metaphorically.

When all chakras are activated, Kundalini is a fiery snake that causes the spine and brain to glow, pulsate, radiate the vitality of existence. On Level 9 and on the rarer levels, lightning sparks from your fingertips; you have the power to inspire others with your vision of a better world. You've achieved the peak of natural realization of humanity and can count your life a success.

THESIS AND PRESCRIPTION

With each increase of intelligence we find in the course of initiation, we gain a wider, deeper, clearer field of perception of ourself, our fellow humans, and the world around us. We look for explanations of what we perceive in human events as well as in events in the rest of Nature.

Completion of our initiation in Level 4 requires that we have a clear grasp of existence. Our curiosity wants an origins story. How did our species gain a monopoly on evil? Does intelligence achieve a conscience at a certain critical degree of complexity? Why and how did our species develop the kind of intelligence we have?

The answers to these questions that I received was a scenario of outside interference by nonhuman entities, a rescue by other nonhuman entities, and a need and pressure to change into a double-consciousness species. Other people have other scenarios, many of which involve Lam, an extraterrestrial of Aleister Crowley's acquaintance.

An old and popular scenario is that of the Book of Genesis, wherein there was outside interference by a nonhuman entity (the serpent), and a curse by other nonhuman entities (the Elohim in their group persona of Yaweh).

According to Genesis, humans acquired a conscience through a case of entrapment. Why would a benevolent Creator place a forbidden Tree in the midst of Eden? How did a talking Serpent find out the truth about this Tree? Why did Yaweh give Adam the prohibition about the Tree (Genesis 2: 16-17) before he created Eve (Genesis 2: 21-25)?

The Serpent told Eve the truth: "Ye shall not surely die; for God doth know that in the day ye eat thereof, then your eyes shall be opened, and ye shall be as gods, knowing good and evil" (Genesis 3: 4-5).

After Eve and Adam acquired the knowledge of good and evil, Yaweh admits: "And the Lord God said: Behold, the man is become as one of us, to know good and evil; and now, lest he put forth his hand, and take also of the tree of life, and eat, and live forever. Therefore the Lord God sent him forth from the garden of Eden, to till the ground from whence he was taken" (Genesis 3: 22-23).

Other ethnic myths contain scenarios attempting to explain the existence of the world and its humans, and the difficulty humans have with living in peace with each other and with the rest of Nature.

Your Level 4 task in this is to create your own scenario and your own ideas for our salvation/redemption.

Here is what I've found that you may find helpful: there is a common thread running through the various scenarios, as though each scenario is a reflection of a deeper history, a metastory whose essence finds a variety of interpretations. It could be argued that a scenario of origins is interesting but not necessary to the more urgent task of putting us in harmony with ourselves and the rest of Nature. If we have an idea why we're a problem, though, we're halfway to a solution.

In creating an origins scenario, you need to explain why we humans lay waste the environment, wage wars, tell lies, restrict each other, beat our spouses, molest our children, neglect the old, the mad and the damaged, and fear death. The other animal species of Earth don't seem to have our problems; predators kill, rutting males fight each other, nesting pairs defend territory, mothers protect their young, but this violence is somehow innocent and necessary. Why is it otherwise for us?

When I first saw my own scenario of the Universe-Eaters manipulating our development for their own nefarious purposes, and then being restrained by our Holy Guardian Aliens, I bought it, in all its gaudy detail—and it made sense to a number of other people, too. Since receiving my own version of the metastory, however, I've encountered other people's scenarios, some of the details of which contradict the details of my own. Since my colleagues seem as sincere as I felt, I began to compare the points of agreement among scenarios; from this comparison, a metastory of generalities emerges, dim but vast.

At some point in the past, our prehuman ancestors experienced an event, microscopic or macroscopic, that not only triggered intelligence, but made us physiologically capable of speech. This event was a mixed blessing, however, since intelligence and communication seem to have unbalanced our behavior and our minds. We work at cross-purposes to ourselves, competing more often than cooperating, destroying as we create.

At some point in the future, we'll achieve a new balance through another event. The Biblical scenario calls for a Messiah, the Lam school sees help coming from extraterrestrials, the E.O.D. is waiting for Cthulhu to awaken, and the religious right expect a physical Second Coming of Christ.

Maat Magick's scenario sees the restoration event as our next evolutionary leap. This requires no outside agent, divine, alien or monstrous. The scenario includes nonhuman entities of many kinds, but none upon whom we're dependent. Intelligence knows its own, no matter the form or level of maturity.

I'm working on the origins scenario in order to reinterpret the images of the original vision. The fewer the contingencies, the closer to truth.

The problem with outside agentry in an origins scenario is that it promotes outside agentry in the restoration event. If we're to achieve balance and harmony in our lives, we need to do the necessary work ourselves. We know what the work is and how to do it; this information is encoded in our DNA: achieve maturity. We need not create outside agents when our own potential will serve.

The original event may well have been the first introspective thinking communicated and discussed among our newly self-reflective ancestors. I'm almost certain that that initial, fatal conversation concerned dreams. Dreams are stuff of Level 9, as is the Akasha; the gift/curse of speech opened the gates of human initiation, the course of which remains incomplete.

The Akashic Record contains all possible information. When we tap into it, we tune in on the particular piece of information we seek. The information is not stored in languages, images, or in any sensory form. We provide the language for the information we receive, crafting images in an instant, clothing the invisible so we may apprehend it.

Reality as we know it grows tenuous in Level 4, yet you must write your thesis on the universe and propose your way for improving it. Yes, it is a trick assignment. Your visions are your own; you will see what explains existence to you. It's a good idea to check with secular science, though, so that your visions can be interpreted in the densest way possible.

You can use your *pranayama* practice to induce a receptive state, then invoke Nuit as the universe. Eventually your scenario will come to you. You must be convinced of its plausibility and probability in the light of secular science and spiritual satisfaction.

Your scenario may well clash, in some aspects, with those of your colleagues. Let the common points direct you toward the metastory underlying all scenarios.

There are many esoteric publications presently in circulation that may agree to print your work in their pages. The technology of desktop publishing may enable you to produce and distribute your own work in an attractive format. You can present your work in lecture-workshops at various Pagan festivals. You'll find your thesis and solution appearing in your art in many guises.

Make the best possible job of it.

LEVEL 3

MASTER OF THE TEMPLE

IN LEVEL 3, THE ABSURD BECOMES THE OBVIOUS AND the necessary. When you come to understand the truth about yourself, your will and your work, you'll experience a reaction of mixed emotions that arise swiftly, and swiftly cancel each other.

You'll notice I haven't written a practice chapter for the Abyss. That's because there is no set practicum for the experience, except to treat your Level 10 body as well as you can—healthy eating, plenty of sleep, exercise, rest and normal work. In addition to inner deconstruction/pulverization, the Abyss often brings outer ordeals of vibrations sympathetic to the inner situation.

All this will pass in its own good time if you don't resist or fight losing yourself. It's difficult to let go, but this ultimate surrender of everything you've built, purified, balanced and honed to perfection is the only way to true freedom. The Abyss experience is not one of death and rebirth; it's stepping off the Wheel of Death and Rebirth entirely.

The traditional grade of Level 3 is called Master of the Temple. It sounds laden with the duties of karma, but it's actually karma-free. The process of assuming and fulfilling the title of Master of the Temple begins when the first motes of the dust that was you precipitate out of the Abyss and settle on the shore of the Great Ocean. This dust is the ash of illusion destroyed by the Abyss: mute, thoughtless, and blind.

It grows into a pyramid in the City of the Pyramids on the shore of the Great Ocean, under the Night of Pan. When, beyond thought, you understand the illusory nature of your identity and all of its possessions, then the wind from the Abyss blows the dust back across the Abyss to settle in its natural level of illusion.

In Level 3, you are an absence, a black hole of tremendous power to change the denser levels below the Abyss, all of which are illusion. Your task is to tend your garden of souls. Ever since Level 6, or even before it, you've drawn certain people into your orbit for varying lengths of time. You've assisted each others' transformations and initiations. Your garden of souls extends beyond the circle of personal acquaintance to encompass the entire human race and all other sentient beings.

In Level 3, your absence permits an unhindered flow of the Tao/ Magickal Current/Truth through you. The people around you either advance on their initiatory pathway or they leave your company. Those who call themselves Magickians but who do not press on in their transformations will find it too uncomfortable to be around you. You understand them too well. Those whom you affect on a global scale will feel your interest and compassion without knowing the source.

The hard-working adept won't need much of your help since s/he's learned to listen to the HGA. Some initiates need more help than others. It's best to ask the kind of questions that lead the other person to discover his or her own answers—the Socratic method.

If you've agreed to help a person with spiritual growth and initiatory progress after s/he's asked you to do so, you must understand that person well enough to be able to help. In crossing the Abyss, you get a look at the seams of the universe and the underpinnings of the soul. This enables you to see behind the details of your colleague's problems, and beyond the manifestations s/he's been experiencing. What you discuss on another person's conscious level must be addressed Magickally on the unconscious level. It's also helpful to communicate with that person Angel-to-Angel. ("I'll have my Angel call your Angel.")

As Master of the Temple, you have to decide the kind and the exact amount of help you give. As a rule, only give the necessary minimum of aid to a colleague, lest you both fall into the trap of dependency and indulgence.

Beyond this obligation of assistance, the work of Level 3 is to deepen understanding of the illusory nature of both objectivity and subjectivity. Magick above the Abyss operates directly in the influence from Level 1, which travels through Levels 2 and 3 on its way across the Abyss.

Magick is the science and art of causing change to occur in the only thing in which it can occur, the dualistic dance of Maya, the world of illusion. Just because something's illusory doesn't mean that it's not important. Would your consciousness have been able to recognize its own unreality had it not traversed the experiences of initiation?

Would you have been able to awaken from the dream, had it not be nightmarish here and there? You may ask: "If I and my colleagues are illusory, why bother trying to enlighten an illusion?" Ah! It's only through recognition of your illusory nature that you liberate yourself from illusion. Even illusory pain and evil need to be healed and balanced so enlightenment may occur unhindered. It's similar to painting or other arts, which are also illusions. One doesn't walk away from an unfinished piece of work just because it's illusory. That would be bad aesthetics.

So it is in the supernals (Levels 3, 2 and 1) regarding Magick. It's a thing of Maya and for Maya, with its success guaranteeing its own disappearance. When Magick works as it's supposed to, both the need for it and the Magickian vanish at the same time.

The understanding of Level 3 applies most particularly to Words, or *Logoi*, personified or symbolized. Comprehension of the essence of Magickal Formulae abounds—all the cryptic acronyms come clear in their meaning. You see how to shape the form that power takes by using the Word most suited to the occasion. You comprehend how to translate Word into action in the most efficient and most elegant ways.

When you cross the Abyss, the nonexistent you inhabits the three levels of the Supernals simultaneously. Level 3 usually presents itself first because of its aspect of understanding; the events of your life click into place, revealing the inevitability of your new consciousness.

You'll notice that the structure of the English language doesn't permit an accurate description of your situation in Level 3. The "you" that experiences understanding, wisdom and the crown is not the "you" of your pre-Abyss life; in fact, you have gone beyond individuality, polarity and union into nonbeing.

Initiation need not disrupt your personal relationships if you exercise proper discipline and good sense. In the early days of discovering Magick, I must have been impossible to be around, so fiery and confused was my enthusiasm. Over the years, I've found that a relationship has its best chances when the people involved share a philosophy of Right Action, have a shared interest in personal transcendence, and treat each other with respect and love. Not all relationships will withstand the effects of initiation; initiation reveals sometimes unwelcome truths. Your first obligation is to your personal transcendence. Anything or anyone who attempts to interfere with this will get "the direful judgments of Ra-Hoor-Khuit." Circumstances can be used in the service of Magick with some wit and ingenuity.

What is it that experiences the super-Abyssal Levels? THAT which emanated and radiated them.

Your individuality's ghost haunts your bodies, animating them with the fire and light cascading from the Crown through all the levels. You are, above the Abyss, pure knowing.

With this understanding in Level 3 comes an immeasurable compassion for the world of illusion. How much suffering could be avoided were all liberated from the belief in their own reality! It is this compassion that tends your garden of souls. At the same time, compassion takes comfort in knowing that all illusion resolves, ultimately, into the Nothing from which it came.

The force of the compassion of understanding inspires your illusory self to actions helpful to your fellow illusions. You have absolute freedom of choice in what ways to do this, since you understand what would be the best course.

Even though you understand illusion for what it is, you're still involved in its processes in Level 3. The involvement is non-attached, however, guided by aesthetic necessity rather than physical or moral necessity.

Your denser but essentially unreal levels act as conduits to and from your new state of realization and the suffering world you've "escaped" from. There's an element of gratitude in your compassion, and a desire to share your good fortune with the universe from which you've been liberated. The reason you are still concerned in any way with illusion is that initiations are cumulative rather than linear. You remember each stage of work in Levels 10 through 4 and the view each level provided you of the world, its operating rules and your own condition. In this sense, truth evolves for you in quanta of different band-widths, with the widest gap being the Abyss.

You undertake the Priestly role of advisor and Hierophant from Level 3 in Levels 10 through 4 as a stage in the process of detachment. It's a matter of tying up loose ends, settling old debts to your past and bidding farewell to illusion altogether.

THE RITE OF THE CHILDREN

THE TRADITIONAL TITLE FOR LEVEL 2 IS MAGUS, OR Magickian. The process of this level is that of becoming Magickian Emeritus, of earning retirement. After all, you began the practice of Magick in Level 10, at which point you were a Magickian, technically speaking. Why is the title specified for Level 2, then?

I believe that it's because in Level 2 you've married your experiences in Maya to the vision that Magick, which deals in willed change, is as illusory as that which it changes. It's this realization that confers upon you the ability to create change in Maya beyond anything you were able to do while you were part of it.

It's enough to make you crazy. Crowley refers to the "curse of the grade of a Magus, and the burden of the Attainment thereof" in his *Liber B vel Magi*, which I recommend you read. In his words, "the curse of the Grade is that He [sic] must speak Truth, that the Falsehood thereof may enslave the souls of men."[1]

Here you are in the realization that your entire pre-Abyssal life is illusion. It's almost embarrassing how obvious it is now that you see it. You have the ability to dissolve into Nothing, but you still maintain a mask—that of Magus/Master of the Temple. You do physical rituals and keep a physical temple mainly as an example for your garden of souls. The Magick of those rituals in that temple is more

---

[1] Aleister Crowley, *The Holy Books of Thelema* (York Beach, ME: Samuel Weiser, 1983), p. 1.

effective in Level 10 than anything you've done before, as are your tarot readings, healings, and invocations.

In *Liber Pennae Praenumbra*, there's a line that reads: "The less and less One grows, the more and more Pra-Nu may manifest." In Level 2, you're abler to remove yourself entirely from your Magick, letting it flow through your levels of density purely and undistorted by egoic concerns. Whether or not anyone sees you, you're impressive; your Magick impresses itself on the fabric of spacetime on all levels.

The impression makes your Word more likely to be heard by dint of the respect your mastery commands, consciously or otherwise. Your Word is your version of truth, of Maat. It's your advice to your species, originating in your own experience, shaped by your native sensibilities, motivated by compassion and powered by your absence liberating the flow of the Magickal Current through you.

Your Word fulfills your will.

The limits of language prevent you from speaking your Word in full directly. You may encapsulate your Word in a constructed word that embodies your formula for success. It can be an acronym like IAO (Isis, Apophis, Osiris), a combination of names and initials like LAShTAL (LA–not, ShT–Shaitan, AL–God), the name of a concept like Thelema (will), or whatever form best embodies your Word.

You may also speak your Word in the arts, expressing your urgent advice without preachment through pure and subtle metaphors. Your example in dealing with other people speaks your Word far more eloquently than written or spoken language ever could.

Even through the most subtle of the arts, your Word cannot convey your whole truth to your hearers, just the parts that illusion can comprehend. A partial truth is a falsehood, but it can be captivating, spellbinding, and glamorous enough to lure the illusions into the initiatory way.

Thus is a curse not a curse when you come to appreciate the humor of it, the illusion of it.

The illusion of theater works because of the artistic compact between players and audience, the compact that the audience suspends its disbelief in the illusion of the play, that it grants the play a reality on a higher plane in exchange for the elegant conveyance of deeper truth. It's the task of the artist to transform the suspension of disbelief into losing both belief and disbelief in the rapture of a new level of experience.

The Magus delights in surprising the garden of souls with direct touches of density changes and novel ways of seeing. In the freedom of the curse of the grade, the Magus comports him- or herself as, what my friend Lady Jessadriel terms, a "mess-cat."

A mess-cat, feline or human, goes fearlessly where curiosity draws it, a Holy Fool in the service of adventure, unmindful of attempts at restriction, delighting in the beauty of the illusion. A Magus, as pure love and Priest of Maat, walks directly into the heart of a dweller in illusion and does that which is necessary for initiatory transformation.

The necessary act may well violate propriety or socially acceptable standards of intimacy, but the Magus is a reality-doctor able to bypass all Egoic defense and fear. A person's illusory nature can be demonstrated piecemeal, on whatever levels are appropriate, in order to create a window of opportunity for initiation. The Master of the Temple is more of a sympathetic ear while the Magus is an instigator.

In contrast to certain older views, the functions of these levels are not gender-specific, in my experience. Crossing the Abyss opens the marvelous clarity of post-sexual gender deconstruction. If you're only reading about this, fear not. Your sub-Abyssal densities continue their functions even though "you" have disappeared in the transcendence of duality.

In fact, sex is better than ever, but there's no longer a "you" to become entrapped in its fascination. There's no longer a "you" to have a gender identity or a political position about it. From your detachment as a Magus (or a Maga), you can use your physical body and its opposite-gendered astral counterpart equally well in concert or individually.

The Magick of a Magus is an order of magnitude larger in scope than pre-Abyss Magick. Not only have you experienced more, including the open secret of phenomena's illusory nature, but you can see the universe as a whole, as the grand context in which individuals participate, affinity groups form and dissolve and where ideas arise and prove themselves in practice. In Level 2, it's easy to construct powerful rituals on any level of focus, from individual initia-tory rites to global workings, with an emphasis on the latter.

As an example of a global ritual, I'm including a group rite that was performed at the Starwood festival of 1992. Starwood is an an-nual event held by the Association for Consciousness Exploration (ACE) of Cleveland, Ohio; the current site is Brushwood Folklore Center in northwestern New York State. There were about thirty participants in the ritual; I'd written out the individual parts on 3" x 5" cards for the various volunteers.

THE RITE OF THE CHILDREN

This ritual requires no altar or tools, though they can be used. The Master of Ceremonies (any gender) calls for the response of all where indicated. The directional invocations and closures can be done by individual volunteers, as can the statements and pledges in the promise section.

The circle dance chant is sung on the same notes as the "Isis, Astarte . . ." chant (see Glossary).

Energy spheres are generated, maintained, and charged through visualization and concentration of will. Their tactile effects are spontaneous.

MC: DO WHAT THOU WILT SHALL BE THE WHOLE OF THE LAW.

ALL: LOVE IS THE LAW, LOVE UNDER WILL.

BELOW: BES! UNIVERSAL ANCESTOR! LINK US WITH THE DEPTHS OF SPACE. SMALLEST OF THE GODS, BORDERLINE OF ENERGY AND MATTER, ANCHOR US IN THE UNCERTAINTY OF BEING.

SOUTH: OSIRIS! FATHER OF US ALL! LINK US WITH THE FORCE OF FIRE. PROTECTOR OF YOUR CHILDREN, SIRE OF THE WILL TO LIVE, CHARGE OUR WILL TO CHANGE.

WEST: ISIS! MOTHER OF US ALL! LINK US WITH THE WAYS OF WATER. FIERCE AS THE TIGRESS, SUBTLE AS THE FLOW OF OCEAN, FLOOD OUR HEARTS WITH LOVE.

EAST: HORUS! ELDER BROTHER OF US ALL! LINK US WITH THE ARTS OF AIR. LIBERATOR OF YOUR SIBLINGS, HAWK-HEADED WARRIOR LORD, FREE OUR MINDS THROUGH WINDS OF CHANGE.

NORTH: MAAT! ELDER SISTER OF US ALL! LINK US WITH THE ENERGY OF EARTH. DANCER OF THE

MASK OF BALANCE, LADY OF THE SCALES OF JUSTICE, UNITE US IN SHARED WORK.

ABOVE: HARPOCRAT! UNIVERSAL DESCENDANT! LINK US WITH THE AEONS OF TIME. FOREVER IN-NOCENT, LORD OF SILENCE, EXPAND US IN THE ETERNAL NOW.

MC: CHILDREN OF THE WORLD TODAY, CHILDREN YET TO BE CONCEIVED, THIS IS OUR PROMISE: WE WILL CHANGE THE HERITAGE OF EARTH.

ALL: WE WILL CHANGE THE HERITAGE OF EARTH.

RIT.A: OUR ANCESTORS, IN THEIR PRIDE OF WAR-FARE, INDUSTRY AND COMMERCE, BE-QUEATHED TO US A PLANET RAVAGED BY IGNORANCE AND GREED.

RIT.B: WE WILL FIND NEW WAYS TO LIVE IN BAL-ANCE, HEAL THE EARTH AS BEST WE CAN, AND SAVE THE MANY FORMS OF LIFE FOR YOUR COMPANIONSHIP.

MC: ABRAHADABRA.

ALL: ABRAHADABRA.

MC: IPSOS.

ALL: IPSOS.

MC: SO MOTE IT BE.

ALL: SO MOTE IT BE.

MC: WE WILL CHANGE THE HERITAGE OF HOME.

ALL: WE WILL CHANGE THE HERITAGE OF HOME.

RIT.A: BLESSED IS THE CHILD WHOSE FATHER PRO-TECTS AND CHERISHES, WHOSE MOTHER NOURISHES AND STRENGTHENS, WHOSE SIS-TERS AND BROTHERS GUARD AND TEACH.

RIT.B: WE WILL SHAPE OUR MAGICK AS A SWORD TO CUT THE GENERATIONAL CHAINS OF ABUSE AND EXPLOITATION: AS A WAND TO INSTILL A NEW RESPECT FOR CHILDREN: AS A CUP OF INNER CONSOLATION FOR UNHAPPY CHILDREN: AS A PANTACLE TO ABOLISH POVERTY.

MC: ABRAHADABRA.

ALL: ABRAHADABRA.

MC: IPSOS.

ALL: IPSOS.

MC: SO MOTE IT BE.

ALL: SO MOTE IT BE.

MC: WE WILL CHANGE THE HERITAGE OF SPIRIT.

ALL: WE WILL CHANGE THE HERITAGE OF SPIRIT.

RIT.A: OFFICIAL PRIESTHOODS OF THE PAST HAVE USED RELIGION TO CONTROL OUR LIVES AND OUR OBEDIENCE. THROUGH GUILT AND FEAR, THEY'VE SAPPED OUR WILL TO CHOOSE OUR OWN ACTION AND THOUGHT.

RIT.B: WE CALL YOU, CHILDREN OF THE WORLD, TO THE PATH OF INITIATION. WE PLEDGE TO YOU THE FRUITS OF OUR EXPERIENCES, OUR PRESENCE FOR YOUR QUESTIONS AND OUR LOVE AS FELLOW SEEKERS.

MC: ABRAHADABRA.

ALL: ABRAHADABRA.

MC: IPSOS.

ALL: IPSOS.

MC: SO MOTE IT BE.

ALL: SO MOTE IT BE.

Chant and circle dance:

ALL: HORUS   MAAT   HARPOCRAT   PERSEPHONE
MARASSA
GANESHA EROS ELEGUA
WE ALL GO TO THE CHILDREN
AND FROM THEM WE SHALL RETURN
LIKE PHOENIX FROM THE ASHES
RISING ON THE CHANGE-WINDS.

Accelerate as the power rises. Begin chanting the Word of Power to climax.

ALL: N'ATON N'ATON N'ATON

Earth energies with hands on ground.

ABOVE: HARPOCRAT! COLLAPSE THE LONG AEONS TO
THE INSTANT OF NOW.

Hold time as an energy-ball between your hands.

NORTH: MAAT! COMPRESS OUR GREAT PLANET TO THE
ESSENCE OF EARTH.

Hold earth as above.

EAST: HORUS! CONTAIN THE WILD WINDS BY YOUR
ART OF THE AIR.

Hold air as above.

WEST: ISIS! GATHER THE WATERS IN THE HOLLOW OF
YOUR HANDS.

Hold water as above.

SOUTH: OSIRIS! SUMMON ALL FLAME TO THE FORCE OF YOUR FIRE.

Hold fire as above.

BELOW: BES! DRAW CLOSE THE BOUNDARIES OF INFINITE SPACE TO BE A SMALL SPHERE IN THE HERE OF THIS PLACE.

Hold space as above.

All point-callers converge at the center, pressing their energy-spheres together until they merge. The MC takes the sphere around the circle as each participant receives and holds it as a sphere of his or her own. When all have a sphere, compress and eat them.

MC: DO WHAT THOU WILT SHALL BE THE WHOLE OF THE LAW.

ALL: LOVE IS THE LAW, LOVE UNDER WILL.

This is adaptable for individual performance.

LEVEL 1

INVOCATION OF THE STRANGE ATTRACTOR

THE 1ST LEVEL'S PRACTICUM IS A FLOWING, A MOVING with the Magickal Current among the events of illusion, seeing and being in clarity and simplicity. Your other levels are attending to the necessary and the delightful, with no need of action from Level 1. You observe and you know.

You see the realm of duality spread before you, from Level 10 to the Abyss. You contain the spacetime continuum, all particles, waves, forces, patterns, and magnitudes. You watch the dance of complexity and chaos assemble the bases of observing and self-reflective intelligence; you witness this intelligence develop imagination, insight, intuition, and interconnection.

You behold intelligence inherent in all things and processes. The universe is a living being in whom the stars and galaxies are thinking, communicating cells, as are planets, rocks, elements, vegetation, animals, people, ghosts, spirits, djinn, angels, demons, god(esses), and all. This beautiful being is illusion, *lila*, the play and dance of Maya; "Malkah is the Bride."

There's an excellent chance that the universe, itself, is a cell of a still larger entity, in infinite regress; likewise, the realm of the very small is a gateway/interzone between the physical and astral levels. The large regress leads to pseudo-divinity without due caution.

You'll see details that I haven't mentioned, such as the mechanics of karma; the possible organizations of incarnations, oversouls, as-

cended masters and discarnate learning centers; shapeshifters, were-
wolves and vampires; the mysteries of physical and astral death—and
a host of others. Dancing Maya is the Great Mandala, spiraled as a
galaxy, beautiful as firefountains and flamefalls, watersparks and
foamglow.

The Great Mandala turns like a wheel; some say the Wheel of
Death and Rebirth; others see it as the Wheel of Shiva's Jagernath;
still others see it as the whirl of the waltz in an Austrian ballroom. It
is a work of art in which we participate as we create it, each of us becoming a vital detail of the overall composition as well as being audience and critic.

The great questions of philosophy, natural science, mathematics, theology, and eschatology reveal how answers lie in the wording
of questions. So many are based on false assumptions and are
trapped in limited logic that all possible answers are incomprehensi-
ble to the questioner.

The details of illusion's panorama you can see for yourself in
Level 1; it's not my work to provide them here.

Your Levels 3 and 2 are present in union with Level 1, distin-
guished only by their titles and functions. Your Level 1 function
oversees these functions and their effect on and from the universe.
Your Level 1 function creates an 11th level of density from the spectrum of all the other levels refracted through the prism of the Supernals.

Tradition calls Level 11 Da'ath, which can be taken as
"Knowledge" or "Confusion." Da'ath is a mirror of the universe
and a gateway to its Nightside, its shells and tunnels, its monsters
and terrors. For greater understanding and wisdom, your three
rarest levels undertake an exploration of the shadow of existence
through the gate of Da'ath. For the best exposition of the darkness that drifts into the levels of light, of the *carcers* (dungeons)
sigilized in Crowley's *Liber CCXXXI*, read *Nightside of Eden* by
Kenneth Grant.

Mr. Grant expresses a dangerous experience in *Nightside*, one
that can be approached "in person" only from above the Abyss. The
gateway of Da'ath exists in a dimension other than that of the Levels of Initiation, within the Abyss and over it, projected as a holo-

gram from the Supernals. He speaks more eloquently on the subject than anyone since H. P. Lovecraft. Unlike H. P. L., Mr. Grant is a conscious adept and priest of the eldrich dark; rather than speak of unspeakable horrors, he presents useful information about the denizens of the tunnels and the dangers of the Nightside.

Once you gain knowledge of the dark, its operations in human life are unmistakable. In the realm of dualism, darkness is the yin aspect of existence, a necessary half of the formula 2 = 0, that by means of which we know the light.

Your knowledge in Da'ath encompasses the Nothing and the All, the duality of illusion and the nullity of reality, the dense and the rare, since the extra-dimensional Level 11 is the sum, reflection and kaleidoscope of the ten levels of density we've been discussing. Even Level 1 can find its essential selflessness in it.

Once your will is fulfilled, there's nothing that needs to be done and no one there to do it. All action belongs to duality, which is what makes the position of the Magus so absurd, since s/he is constrained to act. (See *Liber B*.) There is no illusion-bound duty in Level 1, but you have the relationship of octaves and echoes with your Level 10 world.

Herein lies a great mystery: if you're liberated from illusion, why be concerned with it in any fashion? You can become aware of all your levels while incarnate, and you can work with all the levels through proper contacts after you're discarnate. Physical death only adds a layer of complexity to your work. You could dissolve completely, but you choose continuity for the sake of love, compassion and good art.

If Da'ath is knowledge, Level 1 is knowing. From knowing arises loving. All further considerations are yours to contemplate.

• • • •

I see intelligence permeating the universe, from subatomic forces and particles to the arrangement of galaxies as firefoam ringing dark voids. Light is the blood of the sentient stars, radiating into the voids and bringing life to planets until the stars die. The mystery of the night sky, with its changing moon, wandering planets and winking stars, first drew our ancestors' imagination to the rarer levels of density, to the way of initiation.

A true system of initiation develops our higher faculties to their functional peak, then leads us to recognize the significance of what our faculties apprehend. First we fly beyond the systems we've employed, then we return to illusion to present our own systems.

The metaphors we use in Magickomysticism change as the language changes, as the frontiers of science change, as the human worldview changes. The gods of our ancestors still have the power of tradition, but they are fragmentary and incomplete symbols of the micro-, macro-, and mesocosm. It's possible to use new metaphors in Magickal ritual with good results.

Maat Magick encourages experimentation and immediate experience. One such experiment is the Invocation of the Strange Attractor, which can be done as a solo, with one or a few colleagues, or as a large group ritual. My husband and Magickal Partner, Mike (Lyrus) and I performed it together on Lughnasad/Lammas (August 1), 1991 e.v.

It was adapted for group work by the Association for Consciousness Exploration and performed by about seventy-five people at the Winterstar gathering on February 10, 1992 e.v. It blends tradition with new concepts, bridging different worldviews, and it serves to align the participants with the Magickal Current.

INVOCATION OF THE
STRANGE ATTRACTOR

Upon the altar: a long wand or short staff; sword or athame; incense, powdered or stick; a chalice half-filled with water; a large coin; a small flask of dark red wine; a talisman of thin natural paper scribed in blood or red wine. About the circle: eight candles at the quarters and cross-quarters; a tarot deck arranged around the circle as follows: Beginning at the North and proceeding deosil, place the trumps from Fool to Universe (World), the court cards in rank and in suits as wands, cups, swords and disks/pantacles. Follow with the small cards ranked ace to ten in the suit order as above, so that the 10 of Disks closes with the Fool.

Note: This rite may serve as an instigator of new conditions on the inner or the outer, according to the intention of the operator. If there is a specific state to be reached, it should be sigilized in the AOS method(1) on the talisman; if unspecified change is desired, scribe a spiral on the talisman.

Enter the circle and light the candles, concentrating on the action to clear the mind. Stand at the altar.

DO WHAT THOU WILT SHALL BE THE WHOLE OF THE LAW.

 IT IS MY WILL TO ALIGN MYSELF WITH THE MAAT OF EXISTENCE AND MOTION.

With the sword or athame to the East, scribe a barred upright triangle $\bar{\triangle}$ and intone:

HAIL TO YOU AND PRAISE, O WEAK FORCE OF THE ATOM(2). IN YOUR CHANGING OF THE ATOM'S NUCLEUS, GUARD THE BOUNDARY OF THIS PHASE-SPACE.

At the South, scribe a plain upright triangle $\triangle$ and intone:

HAIL TO YOU AND PRAISE, O STRONG FORCE OF THE ATOM(3). IN YOUR BINDING OF THE ATOM'S NUCLEUS, GUARD THE BOUNDARY OF THIS PHASE-SPACE.

At the West, scribe a plain inverse triangle ∇ and intone:

HAIL TO YOU AND PRAISE, ELECTROMAGNETIC FORCE OF THE ATOM(4). IN YOUR ATTRACTION AND REPUL-SION OF THE ATOM'S PARTICLES, GUARD THE BOUND-ARY OF THIS PHASE-SPACE.

At the North, scribe a barred inverse triangle $\nabla\!\!\!\!-$ and intone:

HAIL TO YOU AND PRAISE, GRAVITATION OF THE ATOM(5). IN YOUR BINDING OF THE ATOM'S PARTICLES, GUARD THE BOUNDARY OF THIS PHASE-SPACE.

Return the blade to the altar, ignite the incense, then carry it to the eight points of the quarters and cross- quarters in turn, deosil, say-ing:

THE SMOKE RISES SMOOTHLY, THEN TURBULENCE OC-CURS. SO IT IS IN THE WORLDS OF MATTER AND BE-YOND.

Return the incense to the altar; grasp the wand/staff in the middle, pacing the circle widdershins, moving the ends of the wand in the in-finity-sign ∞, saying:

IN THE DELICACY OF CONDITIONS OF THE BEGINNING, LET CHANGE ARISE FROM THE SEED OF TRUE WILL.

With the head of the wand/staff, knock four times on the altar. Cry POINT, reverse the wand and knock on the altar: 6-9-9-2.(6)

Return the wand to the altar. Flip the coin. If it lands heads-up, the desired change will take positive form; if tails-up, the form will be negative, or by subtraction.

Set the talisman afire and let the ashes fall into the chalice. Pour in red wine, then swirl the contents of the chalice together. Then say:

STRANGE ATTRACTOR, YOU I INVOKE!(7) LET MY ACTIONS DESCRIBE YOU, THAT WE MAY BE ONE.

STRANGE ATTRACTOR, I NOW BECOME YOU, IN THE ALIGNMENT WITH TAO WHICH IS MAAT.

STRANGE ATTRACTOR, NOW WE ARE ONE THING, THE TRAJECTORY OF CONVERGENCE OF ALL OTHER TRAJECTORIES. SO MOTE IT BE, SO MOTE IT BE, SO MOTE IT BE!

Here drink the contents of the chalice.

Going widdershins, pick up the tarot cards, beginning with the ten of Disks, then the eight, the five, etc., leaving an increasing number on the ground between pickups. After the first round, continue the same pattern, leaving one, then two, then three, etc., using as many rounds as necessary until you hold the entire deck. While gathering the cards, chant:

CHAOS FROM ORDER. THE OBSERVER IS PART OF THE EXPERIMENT.

Shuffle the deck seven times, then lay out the cards in your usual fashion, chanting:

ORDER FROM CHAOS. THE EXPERIMENT IS PART OF THE OBSERVER.

Consider the message of the layout as predictive of the shape of imminent change. Place the significator face up on the altar, and leave it for three days; return the other cards to the deck.

At the quarters, with the blade, reverse the lines of your initial scribing:

North: FAREWELL TO YOU, GRAVITATION OF THE ATOM; RELEASE THIS SPACE; COLLAPSE ITS BOUNDARY.

West: FAREWELL TO YOU, ELECTROMAGNETIC FORCE OF THE ATOM; RELEASE THIS SPACE; COLLAPSE ITS BOUNDARY.

South: FAREWELL TO YOU, STRONG FORCE OF THE ATOM; RELEASE THIS SPACE; COLLAPSE ITS BOUNDARY.

East: FAREWELL TO YOU, WEAK FORCE OF THE ATOM; RELEASE THIS SPACE; COLLAPSE ITS BOUNDARY.

At the altar: LOVE IS THE LAW, LOVE UNDER WILL.

Extinguish the candles and depart.

NOTES

1. In the sigil method developed by Austin Osman Spare, write your desire in a short sentence. Cross out all repetitions of letters. Arrange the remaining letters in a condensed design, inverting and reversing them as needed. Concentrate on the sigil, then forget it. Recall it at a high pitch of energy and release it on the tide of the energy. When you scribe the sigil, keep it folded or face down for ritual use.

2. The Weak Force is responsible for some particle decay processes, for nuclear beta decay, and for emission and absorption of neutrinos.

3. The Strong Force is a fundamental interaction experienced by elementary particles (as hadrons) that is more powerful than any other known force and is responsible for the binding together of neutrons and protons in the atomic nucleus, and for processes of particle creation in high-energy collisions.

4. The Electromagnetic Force is a force of attraction or repulsion based on positive or negative charges of subatomic particles.

5. Gravitation is a force manifested by acceleration toward each other of two free material particles or bodies or of radiant energy quanta.

6. 4.6992 is the ratio of geometric convergence that indicates the rate of period-doubling in a dynamic system.

7. A Strange Attractor is a pattern of orbits in phase space that describes all possible behaviors of a dynamic system; this pattern is stable, low-dimensional and nonperiodic. It is the trajectory toward which all other trajectories converge.

· · · · ·

You can craft a ritual using any appropriate metaphor. Selecting these metaphors reflects your tastes, interests, and point of view; your judgment in their selection is proven by the success of the ritual.

In some cases of group rites, ritual success depends on the degree of engagement of the participants. In this type of ritual, the metaphors should be universal enough for the participants to understand them, but specialized enough to trip their mental and psychic trapdoors.

In other cases, ritual success depends only upon yourself, the universe, and the leverage that metaphor provides between you. Never worry about over-specializing in your private rituals.

The Magickal power of metaphor depends on the strength, the aptness, the tension between the metaphor and that which it signifies. In this it resembles the best humor of wit: if a joke or a metaphoric representation of truth misses the target, neither work. Just as there are lame jokes, there are lame rites; both are a waste of time and both may produce unwelcome events.

To find the right Magickal metaphor for a ritual or for any other occasion, apply your understanding and wisdom. The relationship of significance is the Magickal Link by which a Word can move worlds, a godform can activate and strengthen an attribute, a sigil can manifest the fulfillment of your desire. Traditionally, Magickal metaphors have been animal forms, myths and mythical beings, goddesses, gods, neter, Loa or Mysteries, planetary influences, religious doctrine and imagery, etc.

I find a wealth of metaphors in the annals of science, in current theories and discoveries. For example, super-conductors are materials which have minuscule, if any, electrical resistance. This allows electricity to flow through them with little or no heat loss. This improves the efficiency of the circuit, delivering more force to accomplish work. Even the term "Magickal Current" indicates the aptness of electromagnetic metaphors.

The relationship of significance is a manifestation of the Universal Pattern of Consciousness inherent in all material things, mathematics, the commonalities of survival and development and the tendency to complexity in behaviors and relationships. The traditional Magickal concepts of the Laws of Similarity, Contagion, and Signatures were derived from an intuitive awareness of the UPC and the manner in which all things interconnect.

As in all other endeavors, ritual construction improves with practice.

IN CONCLUSION

AS I LOOK AT THE STACK OF MANUSCRIPT PAGES, I'M sure that this book will be thinner than its neighbors on the shelf labeled "Magick." The reason for this is that Maat Magick is a simple system of initiation that doesn't need voluminous explanation.

It stands on the shoulders of giants, Mages whose contributions to the Initiated Tradition cover miles of territory. These contributions are original works and reconsiderations of older literature and teachings. I see no point in repeating their work in these pages, since it's available under their names in their books.

In twentieth century Western Magick, Aleister Crowley is the most profound, prolific, and elusive figure of them all. Love him or hate him, his work stands in testimony of his attainment. He not only compiled and renovated material of the Initiated Tradition of Western Magick; he also traveled around the world to learn other traditions. At times he wrote directly from the Akashic Record. That's a very prosaic way to describe Numinous visions, extraterrestrial information, angelic possession or oracular channeling. His writings in Class A are channeled work.

Crowley's social persona, according to the annals of his life, was often scandalous, obnoxious, and an ideal target for tabloid journalists and moral arbiters. He often became "the Demon Crowley" to test a person's spiritual discernment and wisdom, and perhaps to provide an awakening shock to any who idolized him instead of discovering their own True Will.

He was vilified and called "the wickedest man in the world" by those who lacked the vision to grasp his work. He introduced a new Aeon of the human zeitgeist and pointed out the futility of the degenerate beliefs and practices of his time. He named sexual prudery and moral self-righteousness responsible for the repression and restriction that encumbers spiritual growth. He aimed for equality between the sexes. Some of his statements about women, especially in *Liber Aleph*, seem to contradict his protofeminism, but they acted to galvanize me into working Magick to prove him wrong.

His own writings speak for him more accurately than I could: check the bibliography.

Crowley's "Magickal Child," Charles Stansfeld Jones/Frater Achad(Echod), was touched by the Maat Current but wasn't prepared to manifest it fully. From what I've read of his writings, he placed too much reliance on simple reversals of Magickal formulae, and on his position of being Crowley's Magickal Child. Nevertheless, Jones transmitted enough of the Maat Current into the world to provide a link in the process of its flowering and fruiting.

The greatest single influence on Maat Magick is Kenneth Grant, an author of excellent Magickal books. These aren't just books *about* Magick; they're books that *are* Magick.

After reading his *The Magickal Revival* and *Aleister Crowley and the Hidden God*, I began to wonder at the general lack of other writings on the shelves that served to advance the High Art. When I read his *Cults of the Shadow*—particularly the chapter on Frater Achad—I knew what the next step had to be, and searched harder for it among the existing publications. Surely someone was working on it!

In a sense, *Cults of the Shadow* prompted my initial devotion to Maat as a preparation for the vision and scribing of *Liber Pennae Praenumbra*. When its source instructed me to send a copy to Mr. Grant, only a sense of inevitability enabled me to overcome the shyness and embarrassment of a raw beginner and send it.

His prompt response and keen interest heartened me immensely. I'd been harboring doubts about my sanity because of strange manifestations in and out of temple, not the least of which was *Liber P.P.*, itself. It made sense to an experienced Magickian and author, one who knew Crowley personally! Words can't express the relief and amazement I felt.

From the initial contact there developed a correspondence that continues today.

I also thank you for reading this book. My hope is that you begin your practice in a wholehearted, dedicated spirit, persevere through your difficulties and attain the completion of initiation.

Life circumstances influence the ways in which you can work, depending on the degree of physical freedom you enjoy. A person who lives alone in an apartment or house could have an entire room dedicated as a temple; a person serving time in prison must rely on astral and mental work. Living with one or more housemates can restrict you to working in your own room, or you could enjoy communal temple-space if your housemates are initiate colleagues.

The situation can be more delicate if you're living in a parental household, or if your spouse isn't an initiate. If there's mutual respect and tolerance in either of these cases, it's wise to avoid making your Magick a political issue by keeping your temple space unobtrusive and your rituals discreet.

If you're living with implacable hostility toward your Magickal practices and aims, examine your will. Chances are, such hostility isn't confined to Magick, but runs through the relationship. If the conflict is with your parents, grant them the respect they deserve as the source of your life this incarnation, but work earnestly toward independent living elsewhere.

If your spouse objects to your Magick, assess your relationship as a whole. You have no right to deny your own calling to personal transformation. Make sure that you're not neglecting your partner's needs, nor your own. Where there's genuine love, there's tolerance, accommodation and desire for each other's happiness.

The four powers of the Sphinx are Know, Will, Dare, and Keep Silent, and the greatest of these is silence. The Occult Sciences are occult for good reason. For centuries, established religions have discouraged and persecuted private spirituality and exploration. This attitude has permeated secular society and is perpetuated by the entertainment industry in its depictions of Witches, Magickians, Voudons, Druids, and those of other paths.

The uninformed still equate Wicca and Magick with Satanism, which is strictly a Christian heresy. It's disheartening to encounter such negative attitudes in family and friends, but it happens.

Be wise in what you do. Magick isn't to be used for bolstering Ego, for creating a mystique or for shock value. Outrageous behavior tends to provoke outrage. Magick is a way of life both serious and joyful, sad and humorous, and always sacred and vital. Speak of the Great Work only to those ready and able to hear.

The future is in your hands, the future of your own transformations, the future of humanity, and the future of our living Earth. Other intelligences await our maturity and other worlds await our exploration.

Success to your work.

NEMA

GLOSSARY

ABRAHADABRA: A Word of Power signifying the Great Work fulfilled, with the numeration of 418. The traditional magic word of Abracadabra is changed to include the name HAD, or Hadit, who is the Secret Self. ABRAHADABRA is the word that begins the third chapter of *Liber AL vel Legis.*

Crowley, Aleister: (1875-1947): English Master Magickian, author, poet, mountain climber, world traveler and Trickster. He scribed *Liber AL vel Legis,* the Book of the Law, in 1904, ushering in a new Aeon of the Magickal Current. His body of writings are a compendium of Magickal tradition and wisdom gathered from a wide range of peoples and times, and should head the reading list of any potential Magickian.

Dialectic: The process in which an idea or entity (thesis) generates its opposite (antithesis) and unites with it to produce a third or more idea(s) or entity(s) (synthesis).

EOD: The Esoteric Order of Dagon was founded on the works of H. P. Lovecraft. HPL's horror fiction broke new ground in the genre, featuring ancient and powerful beings from outer space and from other dimensions. The demand for his fictional *grimoire,* the *Necronomicon,* elicited several versions written and published after his death. The EOD discounted the fictional nature of HPL's work and took it as the basis of a serious Magickal system.

Hierophant: One who leads to Initiation; one who conducts a ceremony. In Maat Magick, the Hierophantic task belongs to all levels of attainment, but finds its fullest expression in the Priest.

High Art: Magick as the mother of all the daughter arts such as science, religion, medicine and the creative and performing arts. Magick is also the High Art because its subject matter—the Initiation of the Magickian—is the noblest work possible for the human individual.

Homo Veritas: The human race with its second, collective consciousness active and functioning. Individuality remains, and is joined by an awareness of the thoughts and feelings of all other individuals. With the arrival of this double consciousness, humanity begins its species maturity. A reading of contemporary headlines demonstrates *Homo sapiens'* intractable moral depravity; achieving our next evolutionary step is the only alternative to self-destruction. Religious salvationism hasn't worked for the two thousand years that it's been preached and practiced.

Hyssop: An herb traditionally used for purifying baths often taken as a preliminary to doing ritual. Hyssop can be found at herb stores. Soak a handful of dried hyssop in a gallon of water for two hours, strain, and add the liquid to the bath water.

IHVH: Tetragrammaton, or the four-lettered name of God. It's pronounced as "Adonai" by the Jews and as "Yahveh" or "Jehovah" by everyone else. As a Magickal Formula, I=Father; first H=Mother; V=Son; second H=Daughter.

Initiated Community: All Initiates working throughout the various worlds, united in their use of the Magickal Current that flows through the universe. It usually refers to incarnate individuals, but includes the discarnate/preborn whose memory and awareness are pursuing spiritual evolution.

Isis, Astarte chant: (with new lyrics from the Rite of the Children)

Jagernath: A large cart drawn in religious processions dedicated to Shiva. It's not uncommon for devotees to throw themselves beneath the wheels to be crushed to death as a swift passage to the presence of the god. The term "juggernaut," meaning an unstoppable object or event, derives from "Jagernath."

Lucid dreaming: A creative visualization process that begins in a meditative state. From mental silence, begin with a seed-idea held steadily, then put it into motion and observe the images that form around it. The development of the images is partly directed and partly spontaneous.

LUTIS NITRA: A Word of Power I received for working on Level 9, the astral realm. Its meaning is hinted at in its numeration.

LTS NTR = 348. 348 + 56(Nu) = 404(law, edict);

418(the Great Work) – 348 = 70(hush, be silent, night);

348/2 = 174(torches);

348/4 = 87(whiteness, sphere of the Moon);

348/6 = 58(love, kindness, grace);

348/12 = 29(to overturn).

Magickal Formula: A code of instruction for a sequence of actions and viewpoints that produce specific changes in the Magickian, the universe, or both. It can also be considered a Name or a Word of Power.

Mandala: A pictorial representation of a spiritual truth. A mandala is usually geometrically balanced, and often is circular. It includes symbols and shapes particular to the force or godform that it represents.

Mantra: A word with no ordinary meaning that's repeated aloud or silently until it disappears. Following the mantra with calm attention into its disappearance quiets the mind and leads to deeper levels of consciousness.

Mudra: A position of the hand and fingers that directs subtle energy-flows in the physical, astral, and other bodies. A mudra can symbolize a concept, an entity, or a state of consciousness.

N'Aton: The name of the personality generated by the collective consciousness of humanity in its next stage of species development. It can be used as a Word of Power or as a Magickal Formula for bringing the second, collective consciousness into manifestation. As a Magickal Formula:

Negate your familiar self through pursuing its essence.

Assert your universal dimensions with your expanding awareness.

Touch with your mind all things apparently outside yourself—the planet, the galaxies, and all forms of life.

Open yourself to the human condition by imaging all humans of various ages, nations, genders, races, and degrees of Enlightenment.

Nourish your DNA connection with all other humans by meditation in the cellular level of awareness.

Natal chart: A map of the planets and the signs of the zodiac as they were at the moment you first drew breath. This map indicates your strengths, weaknesses, inclinations and modes of action and response in life. The natal chart can be useful in choosing a line of work, a life-partner, a dwelling.

Neuburg, Victor (1883-1940): A poet and initiate who was a disciple and Magickal Partner of Aleister Crowley. The two major Magickal Operations they performed were the calling of Enochian visions in the North African desert (see Crowley's *The Vision and the Voice*) and the Paris Working. Their method of working was homosexual Sex Magick. The Tarot Trump of the High Priestess represents, among other things, the Camel, "ship of the desert," a means of crossing the desert of the Abyss. Crowley's "turning Neuburg into a camel" could well refer to Neuburg's functioning as the High Priestess for Crowley (regardless of who was Solar or Lunar) in obtaining the Enochian visions.

No-mind: A condition of consciousness in which the mind ceases thinking and simply observes.

Noosphere: A concept presented by Pierre Tielhard de Chardin. Even as the Earth has a geosphere, hydrosphere, atmosphere, and biosphere, human thought, action, civilization and construction form the Noosphere.

PSI Phenomena: Events resulting from the use of mental abilities usually termed "psychic": telepathy, telekinesis, precognition, dowsing, psychometry, bilocation, etc.

QANESHANTATOR: A Word of Power I received, of general usefulness. Q N Sh N T T R = 718 (The Stele of Revealing). The Stele was a tablet in the Cairo Museum depicting Horus, Nuit, and a Priest named Ankh-f-n-Khonsu. Aleister Crowley accepted its revelation to him as a confirmation of the veracity of *Liber AL vel Legis*, which he had received in Egypt.

Quantum connection: According to quantum theory, any two particles once in contact retain a connection, unaffected by distance and time, whereby one "knows" events concerning the other. Everything in the Universe was in contact at the Big Bang, so everything remains connected to everything else. This is reflected in the traditional Magickal Law of Contagion, whereby any two objects once in contact retain a connection.

Satanism: A Christian heresy characterized by the worship of Satan. Christianity promoted the Old Testament Adversary to the arch-fiend enemy of God and humanity. Certain people who rebelled against repressive dogma and actions of the Church chose to replace Jesus with Satan in their worship. Unfortunately for their initiatory progress, Satanists locked themselves into dualism as the antithesis of Christians, bound in a stasis with that which they profess to despise. Witches and NeoPagans are often falsely associated with Satanism in the media; pre-Christian and post-Christian pantheons don't include Satan.

Scrying: The process of obtaining images and information by gazing into an object like a crystal ball, a jewel, a black mirror, the embers of a fire, etc. As you soften or relax the focus of your eyes, the more delicate features of astral images emerge from their physical components of light and shadow.

Sigil: A design or drawing symbolizing an entity or an idea, usually employing abstract forms. As an example of the A. O. Spare sigil-construction method (pg. 215):

    1. Write your desire—I WILL BE RICH.

    2. Delete repeated letters—I W L BE R CH.

    3. Arrange the remainder as an abstract pattern—

Simon Magus: A Samaritan sorcerer converted to Christianity by the apostle Phillip and severely rebuked by Peter for offering money for the gifts of the Holy Ghost. Legend says that he met his end by falling from a pillar from which he had attempted to launch himself in flight.

Spare, Austin Osman (1886-1956): An English Master Magickian and graphic artist, colleague of Aleister Crowley and Kenneth Grant. Spare also wrote a half-dozen books outlining his Magickal system, *Zos Kia Kultus.*

Sufi-style dancing: Turning in place with the right arm extended toward the sky and the left arm extended toward the ground. The rotation produces a no-mind state. It's best to keep the rate of turning relatively slow to maintain balance.

Synchronicities: Occurrences of events in clusters, bearing a relational meaning other than direct cause-and-effect.

Thelema: The Greek word for Will, and the name of Aleister Crowley's Magickal system. The Will is the destiny of the integrated self; when waking consciousness is united with the Higher Self and the survival instincts, the person can pursue the kind of life for which s/he was born.

Therion: The Greek word for "beast." One of Aleister Crowley's Magickal titles is To Mega Therion, "the Great Beast." Crowley was called the Great Beast (of the Apocalypse) by his mother, who was a member of the Plymouth Brethren sect, and who considered her son to be morally depraved.

Thuggee: The practice of human sacrifice, usually by strangulation, performed by certain devotees of the goddess Kali. Kali, in her destructive aspect, was assumed to be pleased by such offerings.

Trance work: The concentration of attention on the astral planes through lulling the body, brain and waking consciousness into a receptive, mentally silent condition. Into the watchful rest of self-induced trance comes information, in images, feelings and unlearned knowledge. Trance can be induced by drumming, dancing, or the repetition of a mantra. Hypnosis by another person can put a receptive person into the trance state.

Zeitgeist: The general intellectual, moral, and cultural climate of an era.

BIBLIOGRAPHY

Budge, Sir E. A. Wallis: *An Egyptian Hieroglyphic Dictionary*. New York: Dover Publications, n.d.

——. *Egyptian Religion*. New York: Bell Publishing, 1959.

Crowley, Aleister. *The Book of Thoth*. New York: Samuel Weiser, 1974.

——. *The Holy Books of Thelema*. York Beach, ME: Samuel Weiser, 1983.

——. *Liber Aleph: The Book of Wisdom or Folly*. Chico, CA: L. A. Brock, n.d. Revised and annotated edition: York Beach, ME: Samuel Weiser, 1991.

——. *Magical and Philosophical Commentaries on the Book of the Law*. Edited by John Symonds and Kenneth Grant. Montreal: 93 Publishing, 1974.

——. *777 and Other Qabalistic Writings*. Edited by Israel Regardie. York Beach, ME: Samuel Weiser, 1970.

Falorio, L.A. *Liber CXV: The English Qabalah*. Pittsburgh, PA: Self-published, n.d. (Write Box 9011, Pittsburgh, PA, 15224.)

——. *The Shadow Tarot*. Pittsburgh, PA: Self-published, n.d. (Write Box 9011, Pittsburgh, PA, 15224.)

Fortune, Dion. *Moon Magic*. York Beach, ME: Samuel Weiser, 1979.

——. *Psychic Self Defense*. London: Aquarian Press, a division of Thorsons Publishing Group, HarperCollins, 1988; and York Beach, ME: Samuel Weiser, 1992.

Fries, Jan. *Helrunar—A Manual of Rune Magick*. Oxford, England: Mandrake, 1993.

——. *Visual Magick*. Oxford, England: Mandrake, 1992.

Gleick, James. *Chaos: Making a New Science*. New York: Viking Penguin, 1987.

Grant, Kenneth. *Aleister Crowley and the Hidden God*. New York: Samuel Weiser, 1974.

——. *Cults of the Shadow*. London: Frederick Muller, Ltd., 1975.

——. *Hecate's Fountain*. London: Skoob Books, 1992.

——. *The Magickal Revival*. London: Frederick Muller, Ltd., n.d.

——. *Nightside of Eden*. London: Frederick Muller, Ltd., 1977.

——. *Outside the Circles of Time*. London: Frederick Muller, Ltd., 1980.

Kraig, Donald Michael. *Modern Magick: Eleven Lessons in the High Magickal Arts*. St. Paul: Llewellyn, 1989.

Martinié, Louis and Sallie Ann Glassman. *The New Orleans Voodoo Tarot*. Rochester, VT: Destiny Books, 1992.

Staley, Michael, Paul Lowe and Robert Taylor, editors. *Starfire* Vol. 1 #5. London: Starfire Publishing (BCM Starfire, London WC1N 3XX, England), 1994.

Index

A

Abra Merlin Operation, 48
ABRAHADABRA, 167
Abyss, 68, 69, 71, 74, 77, 81, 86, 191,
    193
  Babe of the, 74
  crossing of the, 73, 107, 193
Adept, 15
Adept's Thesis, 183
Aeon of Isis, 4
Aeon of Horus, 5
Aeon of Maat, 5
Aeon of Osiris, 5
AIDS, 42
Aiwass, 128
Ajna Chakra, 138, 184, 185
Akasha, 30, 84, 101
Akashic Record, 188
Akhenaten, 47
alchemy, 24, 42
altar, 11, 35
Amenta, 1
Ammet, 1
Anahata Chakra, 137, 184, 185
Androgyne, 31
Ankh, 106

Anubis, 1, 61
Ape of Thoth, 109
Aphrodite, 34
Artemis, 34
astral bodies, 38
Astral Commons, 144
Astral Planes, 17
Astral Temple, 17, 18, 21, 29, 35, 47
astrology, 24
athames, 127
Atman, 104
Atus, 25
AUM, 104

B

BABALON, 105
banishing ritual, 11, 115
banishments, 115
Baphomet, 106
Bast, 34
Beauty, 43
Binah, 75
Bindu, 139
Black Brother, 73
Black Moon Archives, 100

Body of Light, 130
Book of Genesis, 186
Brahma, 103

C

caduceus, 106
camp out overnight, 53
Ceres, 34
Cernunos, 34
chakras, 40
  Ajna, 138, 184, 185
  Anahata, 137, 184, 185
  heart, 22
  Sahasrara, 138
  Svadhisthana, 136, 184, 185
  Visuddha, 137, 184
chalice, 127
Chandra, 34
Chesed, 59
Chokmah, 81
Christianity, 5
Cincinnati Journal of Ceremonial Mag-
    ick, 100
City of Pyramids, 75
clanning instinct, 137
cockerel, 104
Comity of the Stars, 76
consecration, 115
Consecration-Dedication Rite, 122
contagion, 29
Corpse Asana, 164
Cosmic Vision, 62, 175
Cosmic Vision Meditation, 181
Coyote, 34
Crone, 103
Crowley, A. C., 3, 4, 5, 16, 22, 23, 25,
    43, 60, 75, 91, 103, 105, 184,
    186, 197, 217
Crown, 85

crux ansata, 106
crystal ball, 21
Cthulhu, 188
cup, 9

D

Da'ath, 104, 208
Dagon, 34
Daily Mask, 27, 76
Daimon, 43
Dance of the Mask, 27, 31, 52, 145
Demeter, 34
Diana, 34
discipline rites, 15
Divination, 158
Divine Intelligence, 74, 77, 81
Divine Revelation, 86
DNA, 39
dreaming
    directed, 17

E

Earthing your Magick, 14
Ego, 73, 107
Eightfold Banishment, 115, 117
Electromagnetic Force, 215
element, 25
elemental, 25
Elohim, 186
Emerald Tablet, 28
envisioning, 17
Erzulie, 34
essential Self, 71
Eye of Horus, 22, 170
Falorio, Linda, 88

F

feather, 1
Feather and Flame Rite, 115, 121

Feather of Maat, 22
First Initiation Ordeal, 12
Food Magick, 16
Forgotten Ones, 47, 48, 49, 83, 135
Fortune, Dion, 74
Frater S. M. Ch. H., 91
Frey-Freya, 40

G

Gaia, 34, 35
Ganges Oration, 16
Geb, 34
Geburah, 51
Gematria, 24, 25
Gnostic Christ, 47, 61
god(dess), 35, 37
godform, 35
Graal, 128
Grant, Kenneth, 88, 208, 218
gravitation, 215
Great Mandala, 208
Great Work, 68
Gynander, 31

H

Hadit, 102, 128
Hadit-Nuit, 40
Hanuman, 34
Hatha Yoga, 51
hawk, 104
Hecate, 34
Hermes, 34
Hermes Trismegistus, 28
heron, 104
Heru, 103
Heru-Pa-Kraat, 5
Heru-Ra-Ha, 107, 128
High Art, 3

High Tongue of poetry, 34, 39
HIV, 42
Hod, 23
Holy Guardian Aliens, 187
Holy Guardian Angel, 43, 59, 76, 169
Homo sapiens, 30, 68
Homo veritas, 29, 68
homosexual workings, 40
Horus, 103, 104
humility, 61
hunger, 136

I

Ida, 59
IHVH, 5
Initiate, 15
Initiated Tradition, 23
initiation, 3
initiation
    in Level 4, 186
initiatory rituals, 15
initiatory transformation, 57
invocation, 33
        of the Forgotten Ones, 47, 140
        of the HGA, 169
        of the Strange Attractor, 207, 211
IPSOS, 44, 83, 107, 167
Ishtar, 106
Isis, 34, 61, 103

J

Jagernath, 208

K

Kali, 35
Kama, 34
Kama Yoga, 41

Kathakali, 150
Kether, 85
Khonsu, 34
Kteis, 128
kumbhakas, 183
Kundalini, 59, 60, 129, 185

L

Lady Maat, 88
Lam, 186
Land of Milk and Honey, 103
Lao Tzu, 103
Level 1, 82, 85, 86, 88, 156, 193, 207,
    208, 209
Level 2, 78, 81, 104, 148, 153, 155,
    156, 193, 197, 208
Level 3, 71, 74, 75, 77, 78, 104, 152,
    153, 155, 156, 191, 192, 193,
    194, 195, 208
Level 4, 57, 59, 60, 61, 66, 68, 69, 74,
    76, 104, 151, 152, 153, 176, 183,
    187, 189, 195
Level 4
    initiation in, 186
Level 5, 51, 53, 56, 57, 150, 151, 152,
    175
Level 6, 13, 42, 43, 44, 49, 51, 56, 60,
    76, 104, 148, 149, 150, 151, 153,
    155, 169
Level 7, 13, 23, 33, 34, 42, 43, 44, 76,
    107, 147, 148, 149, 163
Level 8, 11, 13, 23, 24, 27, 30, 34, 42,
    43, 44, 76, 104, 145, 146, 147,
    148, 150
Level 9, 11, 12, 13, 17, 18, 19, 21, 22,
    23, 25, 29, 30, 31, 34, 35, 39, 40,
    42, 43, 44, 47, 53, 74, 92, 104,
    115, 131, 144, 146, 147, 149,
    167, 170, 171, 175

Level 10, 11, 12, 14, 15, 16, 17, 18,
    19, 21, 22, 23, 28, 29, 33, 34, 35,
    39, 40, 41, 43, 44, 53, 63, 69, 74,
    85, 86, 87, 88, 92, 119, 146, 147,
    152, 153, 164, 167, 168, 170,
    171, 175, 176, 182, 195, 207, 209
Level 10-6, 11
Level 11, 208
Levels of Existence, 9
Levi, Eliphas, 106
Liber AL vel Legis, 103
Liber HHH, 60
Liber Pennae Praenumbra, 93
Liber Resh vel Helios, 16
Liber Samekh, 43
literalism, 23
Loa, 61
Logoi, 193
Logos, 81
Loki, 34

M

Maat, 1, 74, 103, 139
Maat Magick, 28
Magick, 3
    of a Magus, 199
Magick Mirror, 19, 21
Magickal Current, 53, 60, 105, 107,
    164, 175, 176
Magickal formula, 5
Magickal humility, 61
Magickal possession, 33
Magickal Record, 21, 29, 30, 130
    keeping, 16
Magickal tools, 9
Magickian, 197
Magickomystical Process, 14
Magus, 197
    Magick of a, 199

Maiden, 103
Malkah, 207
Malkuth/Kingdom, 9
Manipura Chakra, 136, 184, 185
mantra meditation, 13
Marassa, 31
Mars, 51
Mars-Venus, 40
Mass of Maat, 39, 40, 163
Massey, Gerald, 61
Master of the Temple, 191
Maut, 109
Maya, 193, 197, 207
meditation, 51, 62, 102
Mercury, 34
Merlin, 23
Mercy, 59, 61
metaphor, 216
Mooncup Rite, 131
Mother, 103
Mother of the Sun, 101
Muladhara Chakra, 136, 184, 185

N
nanon, 29
nanotechnology, 29
N'Aton, 65, 71, 76, 78, 110
Necronomicon, 221
Negative Confession, 1
nemyss, 106
Neopagan community, 6, 52
Nepthys, 61
Netzach, 33
neter, 1
neti-neti, 71
New Orleans Voodoo Tarot, 25
Night of Pan, 75
Nightside, 87, 208

nine gates, 102
nodes, 63
NU, 104, 109
Nuit, 104, 105

O
Octinomos, 106
Odin, 104
Ogun-Erzuli, 40
Operation Nightmare, 87
orgasm, 129, 165
Orouboros, 109
Osiris, 1, 61, 103
owl, 104

P
pantacle, 9, 127, 128
Parsees, 106
Path of Initiation, 69
Peacock Angel, 107
Phallus, 128
Pingala, 59
pranayama, 13, 51, 59, 60, 183
Priest, 15
priestly rituals, 15
Probability Universe, 63
Pylons of the Ages, 103

Q
Qabalah, 23, 24

R
Ra, 1, 105
Ra-Hoor-Khut, 5
raven, 104

religious possession, 33
Rite of the Children, 201
rituals
   initiatory, 15
   priestly, 15
   seasonal, 15
runes, 24

S

Sahasrara Chakra, 138
Samadhi, 102
Satan, 86
Saturn, 103, 128
scrying, 21
seasonal celebration, 15
Sebekh, 1, 61
self-preservation, 136
Sepher Sephiroth, 25
Set, 103, 128
Sex Magick, 33, 40, 42, 128, 130, 136,
   163
sex urge, 136
Shaitan, 107, 128
Shakti, 106
Shekina, 106
Shiva, 103, 208
Shivadarshana, 104
Shiva-Shakti, 40
She-That-Moves, 102
sigil method, 215
Sign of Silence, 107
similarity, 29
Simon Magus, 23
Sirius, 105
Sixfold Banishment, 118, 177
Spare, Austin Osman, 215
Splendor, 23
Sorcerer's Apprentice, 23
Sphinx, 219

Star of BABALON, 158
   Layout, 161
Starwood festival, 200
Strange Attractor, 215
Strength, 51
Strong Force, 215
Svadhishthana Chakra, 136, 184,
   185
sword, 9, 127
Supernals, 71, 75
Sushumna, 59
Sympathetic Magick, 29

T

table of correspondences in 777, 37
talisman, 127
Tantra, 41
Tao, 60, 73, 74, 185
Tao Teh King, 103
tarot, 24, 25
Tehuti, 61, 104
temple, 11
Thelema, 103
Thelemic Magick, 6
Thoth, 1, 25, 34, 104
Thoth Deck, 83, 145
Tiphereth, 43
To Mega Therion, 103
Traditional Magick, 28
Tree of Life, 9, 25, 109, 158
Tree of Life Layout, 160
Tree of Maat, 104
Trickster, 37
trinitary aspects of godforms, 103
True Self, 67
True Will, 43, 45, 49, 53, 56, 59, 68,
   69, 85
trump, 25
twenty-two paths, 109

U

Understanding, 75, 77
Universal Pattern of Consciousness, 49,
     73
urge to communicate, 137
Utchet, 170

V

Venus, 34, 106
Victory, 33
VIIIth degree, 128
Vishnu, 103
Vision of Sorrow, 75
Visuddha Chakra, 137, 184
Voodoo, 24
Vortex Ritual, 175, 177

W

wand, 9, 127
Weak Force, 215

Wheel of Death and Rebirth, 191, 208
Wheel of the Year, 15
wiccans, 6
Will, 74
willed attention, 39
Wisdom, 81
Word of the Aeon of Maat, 107
Word of Power, 165

Y

Yesod/Foundation, 17
Yezidis, 107
Yogic breathing, 59
Yonilingam, 105

Z

zeitgeist, 218
Zoroaster, 106

Nema has a B.A. in English from the College of Mount St. Joseph on the Ohio in Cincinnati. She has been involved in the study and practice of Magick for over twenty years, was a member of the Typhonian OTO for a few years, and is an Elder (former High Priestess) of the Circle of the Sacred Grove, Church of Pantheist Wicca. She is a trustee of the Pagan Community Council of Ohio, and an Initiate of AMOOKOS (Adi Nath). She lives in Ohio.